IA
Industrial Archaeology

A SERIES EDITED BY
L. T. C. ROLT

9
Building Materials

BY THE SAME AUTHOR

Industrial Archaeology: an introduction
The Industrial Archaeology of Southern England
The Fashionable Stone
A Guide to the Industrial Archaeology of Europe

Building Materials

Kenneth Hudson

Longman

LONGMAN GROUP LIMITED
London

*Associated companies, branches and representatives
throughout the world*

© *Kenneth Hudson* 1972
First published 1972

All rights reserved. No part of this publication may be reproduced, stored in a retrieval system, or transmitted in any form or by any means, electronic, mechanical, photocopying, recording, or otherwise, without the prior permission of the Copyright owner.

ISBN 0 582 12791 2

*Printed in Great Britain
by W & J Mackay Limited, Chatham*

Contents

		page	xi
Introduction			

Chapter

ONE	Builders and Customers, 1770–1970		1
TWO	Stone and Slate		14
THREE	Bricks and Tiles		28
FOUR	Lime, Cement, Plaster and Concrete		43
FIVE	Glass, Iron and Steel		62
SIX	Timber, Plywood and Wood Products		72
SEVEN	Some Major New Materials		81
Appendix 1	The Development of Building Regulations		94
Appendix 2	Key Dates		98
References			100
Notes to Plates and Line Drawings			104
Gazetteer			105
Select Bibliography			111
Index			115

List of Illustrations

		facing page
1	Llechwedd Quarry, Ffestiniog. Slate-making, c. 1890–95. (Courtesy of County Record Office, Caernarvon)	4
2	Splitting blocks of slate at Delabole quarry, Cornwall, c. 1875. (Courtesy of Cornwall County Record Office)	4
3	Moving a block of stone, using an old type of hand-crane, in an underground quarry at Corsham, Wiltshire. (Courtesy of Bath & Portland Stone Group)	5
4	Preparing range work in the St Aldhelm quarry, Box Hill, Wiltshire. (Courtesy of Bath & Portland Stone Group)	5
5	Stone stacked at Corsham, Wiltshire in the 1880s. (Courtesy of Bath & Portland Stone Group)	20
6	Handsawing a block of stone. (Courtesy of Bath & Portland Stone Group)	20
7	Pickers and a sawer at work in an underground quarry at Corsham. (Courtesy of Bath & Portland Stone Group)	21
8	Cutting stone mechanically in a mine at Corsham. (Courtesy of Bath & Portland Stone Group)	21
9	Turning a Bath stone pilaster on a lathe at Box, Wiltshire. (Courtesy of Bath & Portland Stone Group)	36
10	A mason working on Bath stone tracery for restoration of Cheltenham College. (Courtesy of Bath & Portland Stone Group)	36
11	Clay heaped behind the moulding shed, Puriton, Somerset. (Courtesy of R. J. A. Nesbitt)	36–37
12	Old King's Dyke Works, Whittlesey, Peterborough. (Courtesy of London Brick Co. Ltd.)	36–37
13	Brick-making by hand. Removing the green bricks for stacking and drying, Woodham Walter, Essex. (Courtesy of John Tarlton)	36–37
14	Outdoor drying racks, Puriton, Somerset. (Courtesy of R. J. A. Nesbitt)	36–37
15	Split moulds for double Roman ridge tiles, Puriton. (Courtesy of R. J. A. Nesbitt)	37
16	Ridge tile cutting table, Puriton. (Courtesy of R. J. A. Nesbitt)	37
17	A traditional and still fashionable building material. Thatching at Sopley, Hampshire. (Courtesy of John Tarlton)	52

18	Stone tiled roofs, Bradford-on-Avon. (Courtesy of Gordon Young, Swindon)	52
19	The remains of a battery of Aspdin cement kilns which originally stood at Northfleet, Kent. (Courtesy of G. W. Howe)	52–53
20	Lime-stone kilns at Tipton Road, Dudley built 1842 with convenient canal access. (Courtesy of County Borough of Dudley)	52–53
21	Ransome's rotary kiln at Arlesey, Bedfordshire, 1887. (Courtesy of Cement & Concrete Association)	52–53
22	Cement works at Burham, near Rochester, Kent, from a poster of 1874. (Courtesy of Cement & Concrete Association)	52–53
23	The Iron Palace of King Eyambo, 1853. (Courtesy of *The Builder*)	53
24	Iron House for Châgres, commissioned by the Royal Mail Steam Packet Company, 1853. (Courtesy of *The Builder*)	53
25	The old method of converting logs. Pit-sawyers at Terling, Essex. (Courtesy of John Tarlton)	68
26	Seasoning timber in the traditional way, Terling, Essex. (Courtesy of John Tarlton)	68
27	Roof timbering in the machine shop, Railway Works, Swindon. (Courtesy of Gordon Young, Swindon)	69
28	Laminated roof construction in a worsted mill, Bradford. (Courtesy of Timber Research & Development Association)	69
29	A disc of glass made by the old crown process. (Courtesy of Pilkington Bros.)	84
30	Sheet glass manufacture—opening the cylinder. (Courtesy of Pilkington Bros.)	84
31	Casting Hall at Pilkington Bros. Ravenhead glassworks, *c.* 1910. (Courtesy of Pilkington Bros.)	85
32	Polished plate manufacture—'swimming' the plate. (Courtesy of Pilkington Bros.)	85

Line Drawings in the Text

Figure		page
1	Nathan Gough's patent portable steam engine, 1853. (*The Builder*)	6
2	Dr Spurgin's machine for hoisting bricks, mortar, etc., 1843. (*The Builder*)	10
3	Tile making machine, 1843. (*The Builder*)	30
4	Hatcher's Benenden tile machine, 1844. (*The Builder*)	37
5	Early concrete mixer built *c.* 1860. (Stothert & Pitt, Bath)	55
6	Concrete-block making machine, *c.* 1860. (Stothert & Pitt, Bath)	59
7	Patent asphalt roofing, 1844. (*The Builder*)	86

See Notes to Plates and Line Drawings on p. 104

Acknowledgements

Nobody who is interested in old buildings and building methods can fail to be grateful to Dr Norman Davey, whose stimulating and beautifully produced *History of Building Materials* must have led more people than the present author to wish that he had been able to find time to continue the story into the present century.

Of the many other people and organizations who whom I am indebted, I should like to refer particularly to Alcan (U.K.) Limited, Owen Ashmore, the Brick Development Association, Dr John Butt, Helen Harris, W. Branch Johnson, the London Brick Company, Marley Tiles Limited, Pilkington Brothers Limited, L. T. C. Rolt, the Rubber and Plastics Research Association, Dr David Smith, Terrapin International, the Timber Research and Development Association and Turners Asbestos Cement Company Limited.

Much of the time-consuming, but very rewarding, task of digging into periodicals, newspapers and contemporary manuals has been carried out by my colleague, Ann Nicholls, who also took charge of the production of the final manuscript. I am most grateful to her, both for this and for her valiant efforts to keep me to a timetable.

K.H.

Introduction

The archaeology of building materials takes two forms—buildings which contain the materials, and factories, kilns, quarries and machines which produced them. Every town and house is a museum of building materials and every demolition contract is a historical laboratory.

This book is concerned with the materials with which British builders have been mainly concerned from the eighteenth century onwards. It has, inevitably, something to say about the changing economics of the building industry, about its customers and about its labour force, and it makes frequent references to the local bye-laws and codes of practice which have regulated building. It does not confine itself to Great Britain, because many of the new techniques and materials were pioneered in other countries and it is always interesting to see how long they took to cross the Channel or the Atlantic, and to try to find reasons for what was sometimes a remarkably long delay.

Both the gazetteer and the photographs assume that the people who use them have sharp eyes and enquiring minds and that they enjoy moving round the country in order to discover things for themselves. The intention throughout has been to provide not so much a guide book as a set of clues which will make it easier to locate and study interesting buildings and remains of buildings. Few countries can offer such a rich variety of local building materials as Britain, within what is really a very small area, hardly bigger than a single American state, and in few small countries have architects and builders had to face the same range of climatic, industrial and social problems.

For anyone interested in the history of building materials and their applications, Britain is an ideal place to begin.

CHAPTER ONE

Builders and Customers, 1770–1970

Building materials are bought by builders, who presumably know what they want, and any meaningful account of the materials must consequently have a good deal to say about the people who use them. The history of the British building industry during the past two centuries can be written round several themes. It can be seen, for instance, as a never-ending attempt to achieve the impossible, to house the poor decently, to provide efficient, comfortable, easily maintained schools and hospitals, to design houses which are big enough to live in, yet within the budget of the people who are going to buy or rent them, to supply £2000-worth of building for £1500. We may, on the other hand, feel that what we are witnessing, generation after generation, is a struggle between the progressives, who are anxious to bring in new techniques and materials, and the conservatives, who are equally determined that methods and attitudes shall stay as they are. Equally, it may become evident to us that builders, as a breed, are an irrelevant nuisance and that the sooner the whole construction industry is turned over to engineers the more likely we are to get the buildings we need at the prices we can afford. A fourth possibility—and there are many others—is that a naturally progressive industry is always held back by timid, unimaginative governments, banks or building societies.

A few things are reasonably clear. We can list them. Buildings, of whatever kind, are for people to use. They wear out and become less useful as time goes on. Altogether new types of buildings are required to meet demands which did not exist twenty or thirty years ago. There is never enough money, either public or private, to deal with even the most pressing needs, and the growth of population gives rise to a building situation which is never under control, even in the most prosperous and advanced countries. The architect, builder and contractor have consequently had to ask themselves certain key questions, if they are to stay in business.

(a) How can I satisfy my customer that he is getting what he needs or expects?
(b) How can I cut costs, while remaining within the law and satisfying my customer?
(c) How can I secure the maximum profit for myself?
(d) How can I fulfil (a), (b) and (c) in such a way that I can increase my reputation and obtain further contracts?

The man who consistently fails to meet all four of these demands will assuredly go bankrupt, and since profit and new techniques are closely interlinked, only the least successful of builders and architects are likely to resist new materials and new equipment in principle.

Before looking in a general way at how builders have been attempting to solve their problems, it is worth considering just what these problems have been. Who, to begin with, were their customers? This, so far as the eighteenth and nineteenth centuries are concerned, is not an easy question to answer. It is normal practice among historians to refer to 'the Victorian building boom', but now, as in the nineteenth century, this means different things to different people. The nineteenth century was certainly a period in which a lot of builders made a lot of money, and it is easy to see why this was so. An expanding commerce and industry needed new factories, new transport installations, new warehouses, new offices, new shops and stores. An aggressive, self-confident imperialism needed new barracks, new dockyards. A growing civic consciousness on the part of provincial businessmen produced a demand for town halls, museums, concert halls and libraries, together with the money to finance them.[1] A rapidly expanding middle class provided a market for new suburban villas. And, very much at the bottom of the list, were the members of the British working class, accustomed for generations to live under slum conditions in old houses long abandoned by their social superiors or in disgracefully inadequate terraces run up in a hurry and in great numbers by industrialists whose employees were unable to live in the open fields. If the inclination and the finance had been made available to rehouse the Victorian working class, the 'building boom' would have been several times larger than it actually was.

It is a fair criticism that Victorian England's most dismal failure lay in its inability to provide reasonable housing for the workers on whom its prosperity depended. The problem, admittedly, was on an immense, unprecedented scale. In 1600 the population of England and Wales was probably about 6 million and a century later it was no more than 7 million. It then began to rise much more rapidly. At the time of the first Census in 1801 it was 9 million; in 1821, 12 million; and in 1937, 37 million. Growth of this order demanded a revolutionary approach to housing and slum clearance, but Victorian dogmas concerning the poor and the value of private enterprise did not permit such an approach.

There was no lack of evidence concerning the need. A series of reports, beginning with Chadwick's on the *Health of Towns and Populous Places* (1847), and continuing through to the facts presented by Lord Shaftesbury to the Royal Commission on the Housing of Working Classes, drew attention to the disgraceful state of affairs, not only in London but in all the cities and large towns in Britain.[2] As a result of this exposure and pressure, a number of Acts were passed between 1848 and 1890 to make it possible for local authorities to provide housing for the working classes. They failed to deal at all adequately with the problem, mainly because, by following traditional methods and using traditional materials, it was impossible to build houses at a price most working families could afford, despite the advantages of a plentiful supply of bricks, stone, cast-iron and other home-produced materials, adequate imports of good quality timber and a low-wage labour force. There was no attempt at prefabrication or standardised components, apart from cast-iron rainwater goods and firegrates. The terms of the loans available to local authorities effectively discouraged the building of non-traditional houses. The basic notion was and still is that the loan should match the asset. If, therefore, a sixty-year loan period was applied for, as it normally was, it had to be shown that the house could be maintained in a satisfactory condition for at least that time. The ridiculous position consequently arose that housing of a light or experimental construction was not permitted, while traditional housing was too expensive.[3]

A model block of tenements was erected at the Hyde Park Exhibition (1851) and led to societies being formed for the building of 'model dwellings'. In 1864 the Peabody Trust built its first tenements at Spitalfields, in London. Port Sunlight was begun in 1888 and Bournville in 1895, closely followed by Letchworth and Welwyn Garden Cities. Although these were good in themselves, none of them broke new ground in either design or materials, or contributed any original thoughts towards solving the fundamental problem of how to provide working-class people in large cities with reasonable accommodation at rents they could afford.

In 1917 the Ministry of Reconstruction reported on the housing problem in these terms:

> Even before the war the housing of the workers was very far short of a decent standard. In some cases a considerable proportion of the population was living in narrow streets or overcrowded houses or tenements without adequate light and air or open spaces. Many of the houses and tenements were quite unfit for human beings to live in.[4]

The conclusion must therefore be that, so far as housing the lower layers of the population was concerned, the British building industry, up to at least 1920, developed no significant new techniques, did not bring down costs, and, in a literal sense, failed to meet the needs of the market.

Where, then, was the experimental and pioneering work to be found? The answer is, in the public sector, especially where engineers rather than builders were in control, and in certain parts of the private sector where buildings with a new purpose had to be designed and constructed. The reasons why innovation took place so rarely within the housing field were social and political, not technical. Given a challenging export market, the Victorians were able to rise to the occasion and produce something new and appropriate. It was at home that they became anaesthetised by tradition. By 1844 prefabricated iron warehouses and houses were being shipped from England to Africa and in the 1950s E. T. Bellhouse of Manchester, and a number of other manufacturers, were shipping iron houses, churches and commercial buildings to California and Australia, where there were too few skilled workmen available and an urgent need for what we might call instant townships.[5] In 1835 Bellhouse shipped a prefabricated iron theatre to Melbourne. It measured 88 by 44 by 24 feet and it was erected in six weeks.

The barracks and hospital designed for the Crimea were equally

1 Llechwedd Quarry, Ffestiniog. Slate-making, *c.* 1890–95. The splitter is parting a block with special chisel (hammer not visible). His partner dresses the slates to size on the revolving knife machine

2 Splitting blocks of slate at Delabole quarry, Cornwall, *c.* 1875

3 Moving a block of stone, using an old type of hand-crane, in an underground quarry at Corsham, Wiltshire

4 Preparing range work in the St Aldhelm quarry, Box Hill, Wiltshire

ingenious. The barrack hut, to take sixteen men, was made of wood and iron and weighed only a ton. It could be quickly taken to pieces and reassembled and folded into two flat packages. I. K. Brunel's prefabricated hospital was sent out in numbered sections and included plumbing and ventilating units. Similar techniques, applied to housing in England, might have done something to ease the problem of slum clearance and rehousing, but the cost was probably high and the incentive lacking.

There is a basic contradiction running through the building work carried out during the Victorian period. On the one hand, we find a great deal of experimenting with new kinds of structure, especially those involving iron and glass, but on the other we can see a certain fear of these new creations, a feeling that they should be covered up and ornamented to make them respectable, and that the only building really worth having was one solidly constructed in brick or stone. The civic buildings designed by the Victorians were always extremely conventional, with no concessions to new ideas, and the houses for the middle and upper classes were equally solid, comfortable and unexciting. A great many of them have given a hundred years of good service, and it is difficult to ask more.

We could perhaps say that above a certain social line the Victorian housebuilder could provide what was needed and give good value. Below that line, the amount of money available was simply not enough to allow any kind of house to be built by traditional methods. It is very difficult to suggest where the line should be drawn, but, if we take the year 1900 as an example, possibly 60 to 70 per cent of the British population was adequately housed, by contemporary standards, and 30 to 40 per cent was not. With our modern materials, modern construction techniques and modern planning we do very little, if at all, better today. The experience of two centuries seems to tell us that the housing battle is one that we have never so far been able to win.

It is instructive in this connection to look briefly at an industrial town which has never had either a housing problem or slums. In Swindon, until 1945, the majority of people either owned their houses or were buying them through a building society. In 1934, when a skilled fitter in the railway works earned £4 a week a small, brick-built terrace house could be bought for roughly one year's wages, £200–£300. By remarkable thrift and good management the

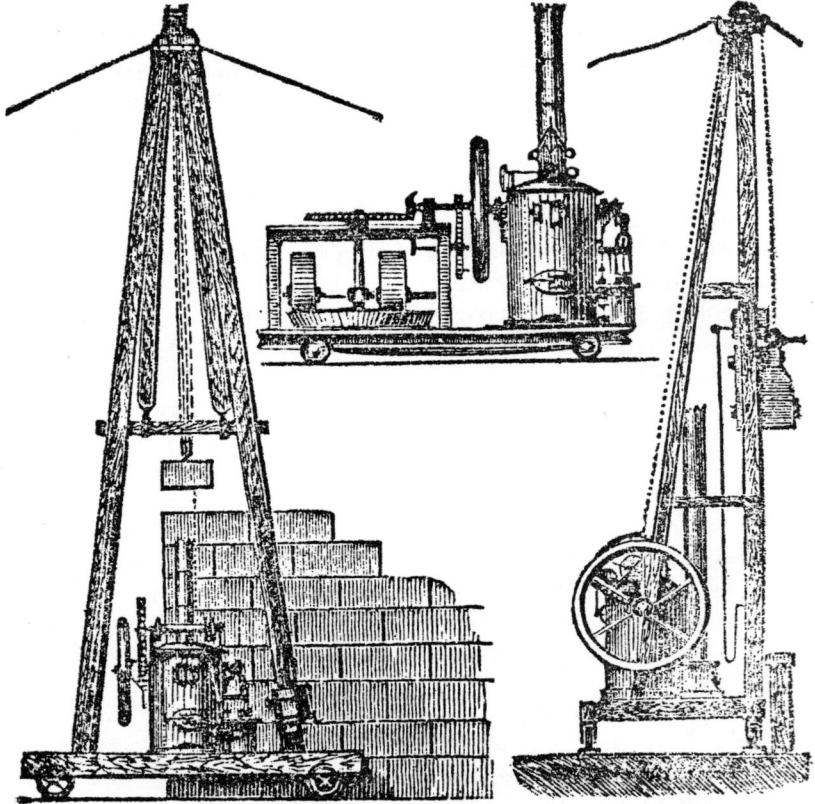

Figure 1 Nathan Gough's patent portable steam engine 'for grinding mortar, raising building materials, driving piles, circular saws, pumps, etc.', 1853

fitter contrived to buy his house. The labourer, on the other hand, earned only £3 a week and for him buying a house was out of the question. So he rented one from the corporation, which in turn borrowed the money from the Government. In 1834, on the other hand, there was no corporation housing anywhere in the country, so the labourer lived in a slum. There was nobody to build for him.

We know very exactly what it cost the Victorians to build small and medium sized houses, because *The Builder* regularly published the results of tenders. A selection of these for 1860 will show the general level of prices. Only the successful tender is given in each case.

40 cottages in Hereford	£1887
Dwelling-house in Hornsey Rise, London	£1320
Dwelling-house at Newark	£785
House at Windsor	£2160
Villa at Thorpe, near Norwich	£898
Residence at Totteridge Road, High Wycombe	£1090
Three houses at Wandsworth	£1498

In rural districts, where land was cheap and wages low, it was possible for a builder to quote a very small price indeed and still make a profit. *The Builder*, also in 1860, instances a group of six labourers' cottages at Parndon, in Cambridgeshire.

The cottages at Parndon (three pairs of them fronting to the railway) are built of white Cambridge bricks (brought thirty miles), with a red brick dressings and quoins, doors and windows, overhanging roof, stained timber where visible and red brick chimney stacks. The cost of the six cottages, inclusive of grates, was £507 10s 0d, or £84 11s 6d per cottage, certainly a small cost considering the appearance presented.

But £84 11s 6d was far beyond a farm-labourer's means.

Not all Victorian building was solid or dependable, however, nor all labour skilled or materials good. An anonymous letter to *The Builder*[6] reads:

Sir—Pray send one of your staff to inspect the houses now in course of erection in, and adjoining the ——Road, Holloway, the heaps upon heaps of old broken bricks (used up in party walls &c), the vile scamping building of these houses, will even astonish you, who have often tried to warn and protect the public against 'run-up houses'. For a seven-roomed house, for ninety years, at £5 ground-rent, the price is £225. You see how heavy the purchase money is demanded for houses to appearance not likely to stand upright (when we see them shored up while still in carcass) for five years unless underpinned. It seems to me such a fraud should not be allowed to exist. Give a thought to the poor widow, who, probably, invests her little all in one of these rotten erections, the almost unceasing outlay for repairs, and the constant complaints of tenants. Again, how unjust it is to the fair-dealing builder who employs skilled workmen and uses sound materials.

Once more let me urge upon you to expose speculative building frauds: I am sure, you will confer a benefit in many ways.

I have noticed also at Dalston, near Hackney, a large quantity of old building materials.

OLD MATERIALS

It is interesting to try to assess the influence which government contracts had on the building industry during the eighteenth and nineteenth centuries. Until the early nineteenth century a number of different methods of payment were found—measured work, fixed-price contracts with individual tradesmen, fixed-price contracts with main contractors or architects, agreed basic payments with extensions and contingencies added as required, and so on. Some tradesmen had no real idea how to cost their work before submitting a tender, and others deliberately put in absurdly low quotations. To guard against this the Office of Works, from 1820 onwards, followed a policy of limited competition among tradesmen on an approved list.

Until well into the nineteenth century the dividing lines between builder and tradesmen and between architect and builder were very vague. When he was rebuilding Buckingham Palace John Nash bought his stone and marble direct from the merchant and employed masons for their labour only. In his accounts, however, he charged for the stone as if the tradesman's margin had to be added to it. Nash, understandably, was a great believer in the single gross contract between the client and the architect, but insisted, as a prerequisite for this, that the specifications must be exact and foolproof. The earliest large-scale contracts in gross were placed by government departments for barracks and hospitals—this had been done during the Napoleonic wars—and by industrial and commercial firms for warehouses.

During the work at Buckingham Palace, the Surveyor-General's officer kept a close watch on what was happening and on one occasion warned Nash that his subcontractors were cheating him, or, as he put it more elegantly, 'not doing justice to the building'. Poor quality American timber had been delivered, the stone blocks were thinner and the window frames and sills narrower than specified, gutters were too small, and lead light-weight. The only solution to this was the one eventually adopted in 1834, when the Institute of British Architects was founded, to have different people responsible for design and execution. The architect was then able to give his whole attention to the task of making sure that his client's wishes were being properly carried out. At the same time, this undoubtedly reduced the status of the master craftsman, and possibly the standard of workmanship[7] by making the craftsman a mere employee of the builder selected for the project.

The measurement of work caused enormous difficulties, especially in the case of masonry. There was no one universal rule of measuring or pricing, and complaints were endless. To overcome this, a custom was introduced during the 1820s to include a table of prices as part of the contract, and at the same time the profession of quantity surveyor emerged from the decidedly irregular ranks of the old-style measurer.

By 1830 the general contract with a single master-builder had become nearly universal for important projects. This had only become possible as a result of having a few large, well-financed building firms available. Cubitts were the leading concern in London. In 1828 the head of the firm, William Cubitt, said that 'having large workshops and ample accommodation for the workmen, there is no difficulty in getting the very best workmen in London, and the best superintendents'. Not all contractors produced work of equal quality. Jerry-building and swindling abounded and even Nash himself was far from blameless. The solidity and excellence of eighteenth- and nineteenth-century building is unfortunately partly a myth. As one authority has put it:

> The deterioration of established building techniques from Georgian standards that *may* have taken place in Early Victorian times has certainly been much exaggerated by modern writers, if only because the worst Georgian jerry-building had already collapsed before the twentieth century opened. Yet poor construction could best be disguised by retaining an established framework of design and using a smooth outer coating of stucco as the house

builders of the forties usually did. Nash—as was well known to the Victorians and thoroughly confirmed by the blitz—had hidden all sorts of structural shoddiness under his stucco; only the skin of paint seems over the years to have held together the houses in his famous Regent's Park Terrace.[8]

The quality of buildings is dependent to a large extent on the quality of the labour force. The number of skilled craftsmen in the building trades has been steadily declining since the beginning of the

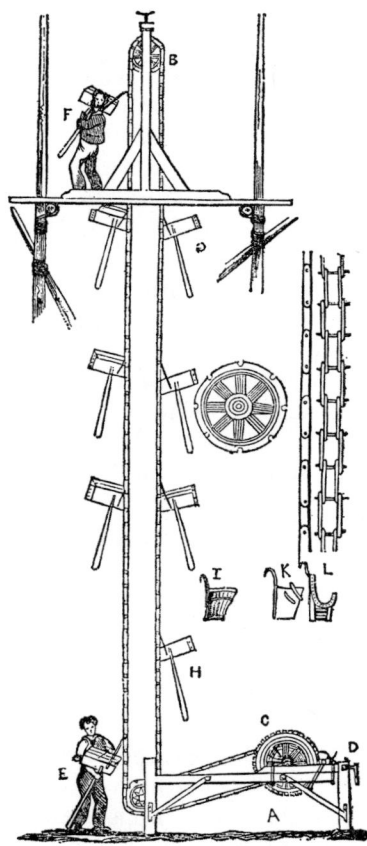

Figure 2   Dr Spurgin's machine for hoisting bricks, mortar, etc. 1843

present century, a fact which has made new methods of construction inevitable. In its *Report*, published in 1921, the oddly named Committee on the Reasons for the High Cost of Building Work gave the total of skilled building craftsmen as 720,230 in 1901 and 365,000 in 1920. Other figures tell the same story. According to the *National Housing Manual* (1923) there were 115,955 bricklayers in 1901 and only 73,670 in 1914; by 1920 the number had fallen to 53,060. Taking seven principal trades together, the Ministry of Labour totals were 429,120 insured workers in 1913, 392,500 in 1921 and 367,030 in 1924.

Considered in isolation these figures are misleading, because they record only the numbers of men who have completed a recognised apprenticeship and who are employed in the building industry at the time in question. They do not include those who were trained as craftsmen but have left the industry, and they give no real picture of the complete labour force engaged in what is loosely termed 'construction'. The actual tasks which nowadays have to be performed on building sites bear little relation to the apprenticeship system. A bricklayer is officially recognised as a skilled craftsman, but a steel erector or a crane-driver is not. A hundred years ago the building labour force was made up of two levels of employee, men who had served an apprenticeship or who were in the process of serving one, and labourers, who dug foundations and carried materials. Today, on almost any building site, the men who have served no apprenticeship considerably outnumber those who have.

It is, in any case, unsatisfactory to exclude from the totals the people who make the materials, components and equipment which are used by the men on the job. The man who makes the bricks is just as much part of the building industry as the man who lays them. To put the first under the official heading 'Other manufactures', and the second under 'Construction' is confusing, if not meaningless.

Nevertheless, for what it is worth, it can be mentioned that in 1965 the number of workers in Great Britain who were officially engaged in 'construction' was 1,747,000 and in 1969, 1,342,000. The decline is explained, not by a decrease in the value or amount of building, but by more mechanisation on the site and by a numerical shift of 'building workers' from the place where the building is being erected to the places where what goes into a building is produced. To give an obvious instance of this, a man who operates a concrete mixer on a building site is, by official definition, a construction worker, but the men who load aggregate and cement into lorry-mounted mixers and drive them to and from the building site are not construction workers.

Even before 1914 it was often possible to earn more in a factory than as a skilled building worker, and since one kind of occupation was carried out at least under cover, probably in heated premises, and the other exposed to whatever weather the British climate chose to produce, there was good reason to go for alternatives to building employment whenever they were available.

Until the First World War, the building industry was mostly a small-scale affair, untouched by advances in engineering and technology, although there were a few large contractors, such as Cubitts. Handwork was still the normal way of building and it was almost entirely controlled by masters who had risen from the ranks of the skilled craftsmen and who each employed a small number of men of their own type. Wages were low, the number of craftsmen available corresponded roughly to the number required, and there was no particular reason to change the system. Since 1920, however, the traditional way of building, and the labour force appropriate to it, have gradually priced themselves out of the market, so that both new constructional methods and a new employment structure have become inevitable, although the deeply entrenched craft unions have done their utmost to prevent or delay these changes.

The result of trade union opposition to change has shown itself particularly in the field of apprenticeship and training. Building apprentices have traditionally learnt their trade on the job, over a period of five years. Until the 1930s only very few of the most ambitious undertook any form of technical study after working hours, but by 1945 a system of day-release courses had been established, so that apprentices could prepare themselves at Technical Colleges for Ordinary and Higher National Certificates in Building. These courses, like the apprenticeships in which they are rooted, no longer meet modern needs, and it has become increasingly difficult to find boys to fill the places available. It makes no sense to train boys to use yesterday's building methods. Two examples will illustrate this. Many technical colleges would like to introduce courses in what they call the 'trowel trades'. Apprentices following such courses would learn how to become plasterers as well as bricklayers and could work at either trade as required. Union opposition to this innovation has been implacable, as it has to the request of the stone-industry for two types of apprenticeship, one, of the old craftsman type, for the experts needed to carry out skilled restoration work, and the other to produce what might be called stone-engineers, men qualified to work in a highly mechanised quarry, to make artificial stone, and to use stone in conjunction with steel and other materials in modern buildings.

The present signs are that the engineers and technologists are in the process of creating their own kind of labour-corps, highly skilled in its own half-recognised way, and that within another twenty years the traditional, apprentice-trained craftsmen will find themselves bypassed and limited to repair work and minor jobs on old buildings, which can, of course, be a very useful and profitable occupation in its own right.

CHAPTER TWO

Stone and Slate

The British Isles contain a remarkable variety of stones[1] suitable for building purposes. They can be conveniently divided into three groups:

(a) the igneous rocks, which have been consolidated directly from the molten material of the earth. From a building point of view, the most important of the igneous rocks are the granites.//
(b) the sedimentary rocks, which are composed either of the reconsolidated debris of the igneous rocks (the sandstones) or of the fossil remains of living creatures (the limestones).//
(c) the metamorphic rocks, produced from igneous and sedimentary rocks as a result of great heat and pressure. The marbles and slates are the main building stones in this group.

The granites are largely made of quartz, a form of silica, which is extremely hard and practically indestructible, but they also contain varying proportions of other minerals which are fairly easily soluble. For this reason houses built of solid blocks of granite are not infrequently very damp, because the rain is gradually provided with pathways through the stone as the soluble minerals are dissolved and washed out. Nearly all granites take an excellent polish when newly quarried, but lasting quality depends very much on the proportion of soluble minerals in the block. All granites have great crushing strength, but this varies considerably from quarry to quarry. So too do their colours, although most of them fall within broad ranges of pinks or greys.

Some of the finest building granite has come from Dartmoor. This traditional local material was used for houses, churches and farm buildings for centuries, but the quarrying of Dartmoor granite began to develop on a larger scale during the 1780s, with the construction of the roads across the moor and, later, with the coming of railways; by 1820 large quantities were being exported, especially to London. The best known of these quarries, at Haytor, provided the stone for London Bridge, and another, Foggintor, was the source of the granite for the prison buildings at Princetown.

A good deal of the Cornish granite was used locally on civil engineering work during the nineteenth century. The railway viaducts at Ivybridge and Cornwood were built of granite from Western Beacon, on the south of the moor, and the material for the dam at Burraton came from a quarry very close at hand.

The only quarries still in commercial production are those at Merrivale and Bridford, but there are impressive remains of the deserted workings at many places, including Haytor and Swell Tor.

On Dartmoor, as elsewhere, the beds of granite are usually very thick. If, as sometimes happens, there are natural vertical joints, large blocks can be wedged apart. Normally, however, it is necessary to blast. Vertical holes are driven downwards, nowadays by means of pneumatic drills but traditionally by using a tool known as a 'jumper', a long bar of iron with a chisel point. This was lifted, allowed to drop, raised, turned slightly, dropped again and so on, until a hole of the necessary depth had been made. It was a very slow process. A series of these holes was driven along the quarry-face edge of the block and then a shallow notch was cut, joining the tops of the holes and continuing round the short edge of the block, at right-angles to the quarry face. A charge of gunpowder was then put into each hole and all the charges were exploded simultaneously.

Usually the explosion threw the blocks over the quarry face, but where this had not happened they were levered to the edge until they fell over. They were removed from the bottom of the quarry by cranes and trucks. The granite was split into smaller blocks or slabs by making a series of holes, larger, shallower and closer together than the blastholes and driving wedges into them, by what was known as the 'plug and feathers' or 'feather and tare' method. Two steel 'feathers', rather like shoe-horns, were put into each hole and then a steel 'plug', in the shape of a thin cone, was driven between the feathers. The plugs forming a series had to be tapped in succession, to produce a uniform split.

After splitting, surface irregularities were removed with a tool known as a 'scabbling hammer'. This weighed about 22 lb and had a short handle and two different faces, a flat or 'spalling' face for knocking off lumps and angles and a pointed 'pick' face, which allowed the workman to produce a surprisingly smooth surface. With lighter tools, an even finer finish could be obtained. Polishing was done by rubbing the finely axed surface on a revolving or travelling table covered with sand, the weight of the block applying sufficient pressure to produce an excellent polish. Sand with smaller and smaller grain was used as the process continued.

It is a curious fact that, although the rock itself has been used for so long, the word 'granite' itself is not found before the mid-seventeenth century, and was not in anything like common use before the end of the eighteenth. On Dartmoor it was traditionally known as 'moorstone' and boulders of it were simply picked up from the surface and carted away for field-walls or buildings, with no attempt to quarry them.[2] Many of these surface boulders were very large and were split and dressed before being laid in position. At some time about 1800 a new way of splitting the stones was introduced, using the feather and tare process instead of the old wedge and groove process. Feather and tare left a series of half-round holes along the edge of each split stone and the presence of such holes is an indication that the boulder was split later than 1800.

During the early years of the nineteenth century, a new industry, known as sett-making, grew up on Dartmoor. The stone was dressed into small paving-blocks or setts, by men working under rough shelters on the slopes of Staple Tor and, a little later, at Merrivale Quarry. The trade was ultimately destroyed by the introduction of tarmac roads. In the 1890s kerbs for Fore Street, Exeter, were cut from surface blocks at Yeo, near Chagford, but the last major contract to be carried out from unquarried Dartmoor granite was for Castle Drago (1911–30), a mansion built by Lutyens at Drewsteighton.

The Lake District has been another important centre of the granite industry.[3] The present quarries at Shap were opened in the early 1860s. They provided the masonry material for the Cockermouth, Keswick and Penrith railway (1862) and for the Thirlmere waterworks scheme (1894). The proprietors of the Shap quarries installed efficient polishing gear during the 1890s and this created a large demand for the reddish local granite which was much used as a facing material for public buildings. Examples of it can still be seen at the Albert Memorial in London.

Granite has been quarried in Aberdeenshire on a large scale for

200 years, the principal quarries being at Kemnay, Peterhead, Cluny, Monymusk and Rubislaw. Aberdeenshire granite went south to provide the material for many important public works—London Bridge, the Bell Rock Lighthouse, and the West India Docks were a few of them. Kerb-stones were also in great demand in London and other English cities long before Queen Victoria came to the throne. They were supplied in lengths ranging from 3 to 6 feet and in a standard width and depth of 1 foot by 9 inches.[4]

The second type of igneous rock, slate, has found three different outlets as a building material. In block form, it has been used for house-building, nearly always fairly close to the quarries; split very thin, it became the nineteenth century's most popular roof-covering; and, cut into slabs, it has been a modish and rather expensive cladding material for the past twenty years or so. The main sources of supply have been North and South Wales, the North of England, Scotland and Cornwall. The North Wales deposits run south-eastwards from Bangor to Machynlleth, and include the Bangor and Caernarvon veins, the Festiniog–Portmadoc veins, and the Corris–Aberdovey veins. In South Wales, slates have been obtained from the Prescelly beds, mainly in the Gilfach quarry, and in the North of England from Broughton Moor, Buttermere and Tiberthwaite and from the Burlington quarries at Kirby-in-Furness. Scottish slates came from Argyllshire, Perthshire, Oban and the Isle of Easdale. Delabole quarry in Cornwall, probably the oldest in the country, has been producing slate for more than 400 years. The colour of slate varies a great deal. In the Lake District, for example, the range is from light green to dark olive green, in Cornwall from blue-grey to green-grey, and in North Wales from green and blue to purple and red.

Slate has been obtained by both quarrying and by mining, quarrying being the more usual. A horizontal hole, the 'split hole', was driven into the quarry face, preferably at a natural joint, with a long chisel and a hammer—the men often having to be suspended by ropes in order to do this—and a charge exploded in this hole, just sufficient to lift the rock. Another hole, the 'pillar hole', was then driven down vertically with a jumper towards the first cleavage. This burst the stone out and allowed it to be removed.

In the Festiniog area there is generally a layer of granite above the slate. The method here has therefore been to mine the slate, by driving in tunnels under the granite roof and cutting out 30-ft wide chambers of slate, leaving pillars of the same width between each chamber, in order to support the roof. This technique, by which new chambers are worked underneath the old ones, from the top to the bottom of the mountain, is known as the descending system. A different method, introduced *c.* 1900 at the Rhiwback quarry near Blaenau-Festiniog, aimed at reducing the enormous wastage of slate by working on an ascending system and using a machine-driven wire saw instead of blasting. By this means a quarter-inch steel rope, moved backwards and forwards by compressed air, was made to take off a 150-ft slice from the face of the rock. This slice was split up into convenient-sized blocks with wedges, and other blocks were then further split by wedges or plugs and feathers into slabs about a foot thick, which were cut into exact sizes by a circular saw.

For many purposes for which slate was once used, such as shelving, cisterns, hearths, paving and the sides and backs of urinals, one or both faces of the slate were machine-planed after sawing. For roofing, the slabs were sawn to length and then split to a thickness of about 3 inches. These thin slabs were held between the knees of workmen, who split them into slates of roofing thicknesses with a broad-bladed splitting chisel and a wooden mallet. The slates were then trimmed to market sizes, either by a dressing knife, or by a machine-operated guillotine.

Until the 1820s neither Welsh nor Westmorland slates were exported to other parts of England. Where they were used locally they were small and thick. It was not until the expansion of the canal system made transport cheaper and easier that Welsh slate began to be sold all over Britain, with the thin slates displacing the traditional rougher and more beautiful material. At first they were known as 'blue' slates, to distinguish them from the 'grey' stone slates. They rapidly found a large market, mainly because their light weight made it possible to use much less substantial roof timbers, but also as a result of a discriminatory tax, during the 1830s, which favoured slates at the expense of clay tiles.

Slates, like stone tiles, are made to a large number of recognised sizes, each with its special trade name. The full range, with the size in inches, is: Empresses (26 × 16); Small Empresses (26 × 14); Princesses (24 × 14); Duchesses (24 × 12); Small Duchesses (22 × 12); Marchionesses (22 × 11); Wide Countesses (20 × 12); Countesses (20 × 10); Wide Viscountesses (18 × 10); Viscountesses (18 × 9); Wide Ladies (16 × 10); Broad Ladies (16 × 9); Ladies (16 × 8); Wide Headers (14 × 12); Small Headers (13 × 10); Doubles (13 × 7); Wide Doubles (12 × 8); Small Doubles (12 × 6); Singles (10 × 8); Units (10 × 6).

Stone tiles have been used in Britain since Roman times. They are made from certain types of limestone and sandstone which split naturally into ½ to 1 inch thicknesses. These are found in many areas, ranging from the hard siliceous sandstone of the Lower Purbeck beds in Dorset to the sandy limestone at Collyweston, in Lincolnshire. The most important workings for stone tiles were at Stonesfield, near Charlbury in Oxfordshire, where the beds extended over an area of more than two square miles. The slabs of stone there were laid out flat on the ground after being taken from the quarry and left until the frost started to split them, after which they were trimmed to shape and a hole picked out at the top, so that they could be hung to the roof by broad-headed nails or oak pegs.

These stone tiles were graduated in length from 5 inches to 23 inches, and in thickness from an inch to half an inch. They were laid so that the smallest sizes were at the top of the roof and the largest at the bottom, a custom which had the double effect of improving the appearance of the roof and also of reducing the weight towards the ridge. Even so, the total weight on a stone-tiled roof was enormous and the timbers had to be very stout to take it. Few stone tiles have been made since 1939 and quantities of secondhand tiles in good condition fetch very good prices nowadays, especially in the fashionable Cotswold district.

Both limestones and sandstones are found in great variety within the British Isles. Sandstones of building quality have been quarried in South Devon, South Somerset, South and West Lancashire, and the North Midlands, with a narrow belt of the much-prized millstone running up the centre of England and covering part of East Lancashire and West Yorkshire. The limestones range from the white limestone of Portland to the magnesian limestone of Yorkshire and from the compact, hard Kentish ragstone to the carboniferous limestones of Cumberland and Yorkshire. Until the late eighteenth century, when canals brought about farreaching changes in the inland transport of heavy, bulky freight, builders would normally use a local stone, unless an easy route by sea or river were available.

The industrial towns of Lancashire, for example, were built to a great extent of the sandstones and gritstones which occur abundantly within the county. They are not always easy to work and their wearing qualities vary a great deal, but they had the advantage of being ready to hand and cheap, so there could be little argument about using them. The paving stones, flags and building stones from the quarries near Haslingden, Rawtenstall, Bacup and Whitworth made the pavements, the floors and the walls of factories, town halls, and workers' houses, lined the railway cuttings and went into the bridges and viaducts. Flagstones from the Dalton quarries were used in the Walker Art Gallery and St George's Hall, in Liverpool, without any feeling that the prestige of the building was being reduced in any way by making use of ordinary local materials. What could only be discovered by experience, however, was how well or how badly a local stone, well tested and successful in villages and in clean country air, would cope with the soot and sulphur of a heavily industrialised area. A stone had to be assumed satisfactory until it was proved otherwise and, in any case, it was only with the coming of railways that there was anything like a free choice of stones, at least for expensive buildings, practically everywhere in Britain, and by that time it had become all too obvious which were the good wearing stones and which were not.

It should be remembered, however, that until about 1600 the total amount of stone quarried each year was very small, compared with the great quantities needed during the seventeenth, eighteenth and nineteenth centuries. It was the exploitation of the freestone beds of first Portland and then the Bath district which transformed the scale of the stone industry. There were a number of related reasons for this—the need to rebuild much of London after the Great Fire, the commissioning of a very large number of public buildings, and the increase in the national wealth which made it possible to consider more comfortable and more elegant private houses.

The greatly increased demand for Portland stone during the seventeenth century caused prices to fall by 50 per cent between 1630 and 1700. By then the Portland quarrymen were among the best paid in Britain and continued to be in this fortunate position throughout the eighteenth century. Their productivity was high for the times, despite the amount of work that had to be carried out before they reached the freestone beds. The whitbed, the best stone

5 Stone stacked at Corsham, Wiltshire, in the 1880s

6 Handsawing a block of stone

7 Pickers and a sawer at work in an underground quarry at Corsham

8 Cutting stone mechanically in a mine at Corsham

for external use, lies about 35 feet below the surface. It is a hard, crystalline stone, with excellent weathering qualities. Immediately above it is the roach-bed, a very hard, amber-coloured stone, for which there was no commercial use until the 1930s, when diamond-tipped saws allowed it to be converted into slabs. Before that it was blasted off with explosives and used, if at all, as a filling material for breakwaters. The whitbed is 8 to 10 feet thick. Below it is the much softer basebed, which cannot be safely used for external work.

In 1812 there were 800 men and boys employed in the Portland quarries. They produced about 25,000 tons of saleable stone a year, which meant that Portland stone was a scarce commodity. 'There was competition to get it and, once obtained, it had to be used economically.'[5] It was much the best stone to use in cities, but it was made artificially expensive by the duty which had to be paid to the Crown for each ton removed from the island. Even so, builders held it in the highest regard and their important clients were usually willing to pay a good price for it.

> Its hardness (said a building manual of the 1820s) gives it many requisites for producing excellent masonry. Most of our public buildings are composed entirely of this stone, and it is frequently made use of in dwelling houses for kirbs, strings fascias, columns, cornices, floors of halls, vestibules, stair cases, &c. The Portland free-stone is decidedly the most handsome free-stone known, being capable of bearing an arris in moulding equal to marble, but the great expense of the freight and duty has lately made the Gloucestershire stone its competitor; and it will, perhaps, in a few years be entirely superseded thereby, except for internal work, where its superior neatness will always gain it preference.[6]

'The Gloucestershire stone' was, in fact, Bath stone, and the Victorian building boom ensured that the market was able to absorb the output of both the Portland and the Bath quarries without any great difficulty. The real beginning of the Bath stone industry was in 1727, when the Avon navigation was completed, allowing stone to be sent by barge to Bristol and from there by ship. The development of the Combe Down quarries by Ralph Allen followed soon afterwards. Allen was a stone entrepreneur, whose chief aim was to bring down the price of Bath stone and in this way to undercut the market. To achieve this he organised and housed his labour force with remarkable efficiency, built a railway to get stone down from the quarries to the wharf on the Avon, and created a steady, regular flow of work. The Portland interests met this unwelcome competition with great energy and ingenuity. They were determined to have the London market to themselves. As John Wood reported:

> The introduction of Free Stone into London met with great opposition; some of the Opponents maliciously comparing it to Cheshire Cheese, liable to breed Maggots that would soon Devour it; and the late Mr. Colen Campbell, as Architect, together with the late Messeurs Hawksmoor and James, as Clerks of the Works of Greenwich Hospital, were so prejudiced against it that at a Publick Meeting of the Governors of that Building at Salters Hall, in the spring of the Year 1728, they Represented it as a Material unable to bear any Weight, of a Coarse Texture, bad colour, and almost as dear as Portland Stone for a Publick Work in or near London.[7]

Nevertheless the demand for Bath stone grew steadily, partly, no doubt, as a result of the splendid new houses erected in Bath itself. The Circus, Royal Crescent and Pulteney Street were a constant advertisement for the product of the local quarries. In 1810 the market was greatly extended by the opening of the Kennet and Avon Canal. After that date Bath stone could be delivered in Oxford, for example, for only a penny a ton-mile. The Great Western Railway from Paddington to Bristol was completed in 1841. It killed the Kennet and Avon, but allowed Bath stone to be delivered cheaply to any part of Britain.

The 1856 catalogue of one of the larger Bath quarry firms, Randall and Saunders, quotes prices per foot cube for stone delivered to any railway station in Britain. For Combe Down stone some examples are: Birmingham 1s 1d, Brighton 1s 5d, Leeds 1s 7d, London 1s 1d, Manchester 1s 9d.

By the 1850s a high proportion of Bath stone was being taken not from quarries but from mines, in the Box and Corsham areas. Several companies in the area were amalgamated in 1887, to form the Bath Stone Firms Limited. In the first year of operations the new group quarried 1,501,084 cubic feet of stone and sold nearly all of it.

By the turn of the century 3 million cubic feet were quarried each year and in 1899 the Bath Stone Firms took over the Portland quarries, giving the company control over most of the British output of building limestone. It reached nearly a monopoly position in the 1930s, with the acquisition of the quarries at Beer, in Devon, Ham Hill and Doulting in Somerset and, most important of all, Clipsham in Rutland.

In the nineteenth century production at the three Rutland quarrying areas, Ketton, Little Castleton and Clipsham, was greatly increased. Another quarry, at Edith Weston, was also important. It provided large quantities of its very fine-grained stone for churches, banks and hotels in the Midlands. In 1839 the Crown Commissioners, in their *Report on Building Stones for the new House of Commons*, thought very highly of Ketton stone, emphasising its 'great cohesive strength and high specific quality'. Before the coming of the railways, it was expensive, however, costing 1s 9d a cubic foot at the quarries and 3s 4d delivered in London.

Clipsham quarries supplied stone for Windsor Castle in 1360 but, like Ketton, Clipsham came into its own in the nineteenth century, when it was extensively used in both Oxford and Cambridge for new building and refacing. The Victorian architects inherited the results of the errors of their predecessors and they made a good many mistakes themselves, which have had to be put right in recent years. Most of the decay in stone buildings has been due to the choice of a stone which was unsuitable for a smoke-laden town atmosphere, to careless or ignorant selection of stone at the quarry, or, a very common Victorian failing, to the use of iron clamps in the masonry, which rusted and destroyed the stone. When it came to stone, the Victorians were in one way perfectionists and in another incredibly stupid and shortsighted. Bath stone was their undoing. It was so easy to work that the joints between the individual stones could be rubbed down to give a very tight fit, which looked well but made it impossible to work in enough mortar between the stones to hold them together. Iron clamps were therefore used to do the job that mortar should have done, with the disastrous results indicated above. Clipsham presented similar temptations and, in the hands of a Victorian builder, not infrequently came out looking like modern walls of reconstituted stone.

The method of quarrying limestone varies considerably. Where, as in the case of Keinton stone, it occurs near the surface in thin, well-defined horizontal beds, with good natural joints, little more has to be done than to lever it out with crowbars and lift it to the surface. Quarries of this type are worked in floors, rather than faces. The various Bath stones, on the other hand, are mined. They occur in steep beds, up to 22 feet thick, which have to be reached by shafts or inclines. Pillars of stone were left to support the roof as the excavation proceeded. Between the freestone and the roof, a thin layer was taken out with picks. This allowed a vertical cut to be made downwards from the roof to the base of the bed. A second cut was made at an angle to the first, removing a V-shaped groove into which a man could just squeeze, in order to cut along the back of the block. A third vertical cut separated the block, which could then be levered out and lifted by cranes on to trollies running on rails to the exit of the mine.

The blocks of stone from some of the mines in the Bath area had to be kept underground during the winter months until all danger from frost had gone. If it had been taken up immediately, the water in the stone would have frozen and the stone would have split.

Since 1945 Bath stone from the Monks Park mine, the only one now in operation, has been cut mechanically by means of 'Samson' coal-cutting machines, which do the job efficiently, but make a very wide cut, so that the amount of wastage is considerable.

The other British limestones, including those at Portland and Clipsham, in Rutland, have all been worked in open quarries, by levering and wedging. Blasting has been used for some of the sandstones, where the stone occurs in rock masses, rather than in distinct beds. Some sandstones have been extracted in very large blocks. The Bothwell Park quarries on Lanarkshire have supplied stone in blocks of up to 10 tons in weight, with a thickness of 5 feet.

The variety of sandstones is so great that some are not recognised as sandstones at all by the average lay observer, who can easily be confused by their hardness and colour. The Blue Pennant stone, quarried for many years at Fishponds, on the outskirts of Bristol, and found in many local houses, is a deep blue colour, sometimes verging on purple. It is very hard and difficult to work, and consequently expensive. The Forest of Dean stone is also a good durable sandstone, although not quite as hard as Bristol Pennant. Its colours include blues, greys and browns, one often shading into another in the same block. Victorian and Edwardian builders made much use of it for the construction of bridges and docks. Avonmouth Docks, for instance, contains a great deal of it.

The thin-bedded, laminated sandstones from Yorkshire, particularly from South Owram quarry, have been very popular for paving slabs, steps and landings. On the London market, during the nineteenth century, the term 'York Stone' came to be almost synonymous with 'sandstone', which was very confusing, since the range of quality and colour was very wide.

One of the strangest sandstone formations in the British Isles occurs at Liscannor, County Clare. This stone, a grey millstone grit, marketed between about 1880 and 1910 under the trade name of 'Shamrock'. The stone lies in regular-shaped blocks, which have the appearance of being sawn and planed. The bed is absolutely horizontal, so that it was easy to produce flagstones and steps with perfectly true natural faces.

The evidence of the immense amount of stone taken from the major quarries during the eighteenth and nineteenth centuries is impressive. The great Craigleith quarries, near Edinburgh, for example, produced one of the best sandstones in Britain. It was used for nearly all the principal buildings in Edinburgh, and for many in London, including the piers of Southwark Bridge. On Portland one can see not only the vast quarries themselves but, even more interesting, a great deal of quarried stone that was never used. This unsold stone, although perfectly sound, is of second quality. Until the outbreak of war in 1939 most architects bought Portland stone as a package, with some of top quality and the rest containing slight streaking, caused by the presence of metallic oxides or decomposed vegetable matter. The best quality stone was used nearer the ground and the remainder higher up on the building, a very satisfactory and reasonable arrangement. After the war, however, it became possible to buy only selected stone. Architects came to inspect this, the second quality was then difficult to sell and the first quality had to be priced up in consequence, so producing an unnecessary restriction of the market.

A further problem, in some ways more serious, was caused by the introduction of the concrete block as the normal material for party walls. Before this, in the stone areas, the tradition had been to use smaller pieces of dressed stone for gardens and internal party walling and to work in rubble behind the ashlar facing of the building. Rubble, with dressed quoins and door and window surrounds, was also the normal way of facing the houses of the poor. This thrifty system allowed almost the whole output of the quarry to be sold. Once it broke down, and for this the concrete block was very largely responsible, the economy of the industry was undermined. The dressed stone had to carry all the overheads of the quarry and inevitably became an expensive luxury product. To some extent a new market has been found for the small pieces and the second grade material by grinding them up to form an aggregate for facing up concrete blocks, so producing what is now known as reconstituted or reconstructed stone, but the modern outlet is not the equivalent of the old one, because today's block has the Bath, Portland or other freestone in only part of its thickness.

The vast stone mines at Box and Corsham in Wiltshire remain to show what the scale of the block-stone industry once was; in the days when load-bearing stonework was normal. Only one of these mines, Monks Park, is now in operation. Using mechanical cutters, a dozen men produce as much stone as five times that number did before 1939.

If natural stone has a future in the construction of new buildings it must lie in more mass-production and in acceptable techniques which allow ashlar facing to be easily and efficiently attached to steel or reinforced concrete frames. Stone must, in other words, be able to compete with other cladding materials. This has already been achieved—it is a form of stone engineering—in a number of large buildings. The Carlton Tower Hotel and the headquarters of Guest, Keen and Nettlefold, both in London, and the extension to Queens' Colledge, Cambridge, are good examples.

Experiments are also being made with very large panels of stone, prefabricated from standard modules and held together with prestressed wires. The whole slab, measuring perhaps 10 ft by 6 ft, can be transported direct from the factory to the site and fixed very rapidly to the face of the building.

A good deal of attention has also been paid to increasing the fashion-appeal of natural stone by cutting patterns into the face. This patterning, by means of machine-cut grooves, provides a great variety of designs and textures. Stones with a strongly defined natural pattern can be used for the same purpose. Very coarse roach, usually polished, and shelly whitbed are in particular demand for this type of work.

It would be fair to say that the future of the British stone industry depends on its engineers and its salesmen, very much as the development of the Bath stone industry in the eighteenth century depended on the showmanship, organising ability and selling genius of Ralph Allen.

CHAPTER THREE

Bricks and Tiles

'The manufacture of burnt bricks,' as Norman Davey has pointed out, 'was a lengthy process which could only be carried out efficiently under settled social and political conditions, in which buildings of a permanent character needing the products could be erected.'[1] In Britain, very little brickmaking was carried on after the break-up of the Roman Empire, although some Saxon and Norman churches re-used bricks recovered from the ruins of Roman buildings. There was a revival of brickmaking in East Anglia during the first half of the thirteenth century, almost certainly as a result of trading connections with the Netherlands. These new bricks were much larger than those used today. They were usually between $10\frac{1}{4}$ and $12\frac{1}{2}$ inches long, 5 to 6 inches wide and $1\frac{3}{4}$ to $2\frac{3}{4}$ inches thick, although occasionally, as at Waltham Abbey (1370) they were as large as 15 inches long and $7\frac{1}{2}$ inches wide. This size of brick was known as the 'Great' brick and was made in the eastern counties until the beginning of the sixteenth century.

In about 1350 a smaller brick began to be imported from the Netherlands and was soon being made in England. It was approximately 6 to $8\frac{1}{4}$ inches long, 3 to $3\frac{3}{4}$ inches wide and $1\frac{3}{4}$ to $2\frac{1}{4}$ inches thick. From the fifteenth century onwards some Dutch bricks of an even smaller size were imported, 6 to $8\frac{1}{4}$ inches long, 3 to $3\frac{3}{4}$ inches wide and $1\frac{3}{8}$ to $1\frac{3}{4}$ inches thick.

Much fine brickwork of the fifteenth and sixteenth centuries survives. Examples are to be found at Hurstmonceux (1449), the Bishop's Palace, Hatfield (1480), Layer Marney Towers, Essex, (1500–25), Hampton Court (1515–30) and Compton Wynyates, Warwickshire (1520). Some of the Tudor brickwork was very elaborate, with moulding, carving and patterning. Excellent work of this kind can be seen at St Osyth's Priory, Essex (1475). Most Tudor brickwork has fairly thick mortar joints, partly to reduce costs and partly because the bricks themselves were not very regular in size or shape. By the seventeenth century the technique of brickmaking had greatly improved and the joints became much thinner.

Until the eighteenth century brickmakers and builders were left more or less to their own devices, with very little attempt at government control, but during the reign of George III the introduction of a brick tax (1784) changed the situation in two important ways; bricks became larger, since a large brick paid the same tax as a small one, and tile-hung walls became popular, since tiles escaped the tax. One of the manufacturers who turned to large bricks in 1794, as a result of the tax was Sir Joseph Wilkes who had a brickworks at Measham in Leicestershire. His large bricks, made twice the normal size, were known locally as Wilkes' Gobs. A row of cottages, known as the Brickyards, was built of these bricks and can still be seen, although the brickwork itself disappeared long ago. Examples of Wilkes' Gobs are also to be seen in other buildings in Measham and in Ashby-de-la-Zouch.[2]

In 1803, however, tiles were taxed and bricks larger than 10 by 3 by 5 inches paid double the tax, and after this the size settled down to 9 by $4\frac{1}{2}$ by 3 inches, rather larger than the modern standard.

The rate of duty was substantial. In 1784 it was 2s 6d a 1000 on all bricks. This was raised to 4s a 1000 in 1794 and in 1803 to 5s for the smaller bricks and 10s for the larger. The 1803 schedule also included these provisions:

For every thousand of bricks which shall be made in Great Britain, and which shall be smoothed or polished on one or more side or sides, the same not exceeding the superficial dimensions of ten inches long by five inches wide	12	0
For every thousand of plain tiles which shall be made in Great Britain	4	10
For every thousand of pan or ridge tiles which shall be made in Great Britain	12	10
For every hundred of paving tiles which shall be made in Great Britain not exceeding ten inches square	2	5
For every hundred of paving tiles which shall be made in Great Britain exceeding ten inches square	4	10

In 1833 the duties on tiles were wholly repealed and in 1835 the duty on bricks was again raised, making the duty on common bricks 5s 10d a thousand. By a strange oversight, this Act, which was intended to put roofing tiles on the same basis as slates, also repealed the duties on paving tiles, although ordinary bricks used for paving remained subject to duty as before. If, however, the bricks measured 10 inches by 10 inches they were classified as tiles and no duty was payable. A new Act of 1839 put a uniform duty of 5s 10d a thousand on all bricks of which the cubic content did not exceed 150 cubic inches, no matter what the shape or quality. All taxes on bricks and tiles were removed in 1850.

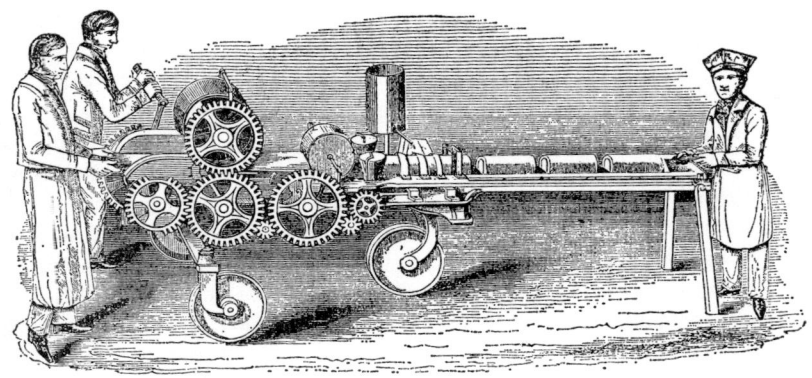

Figure 3   Tile making machine, 1843. The clay is being fed into the machine in the form of a thin slab

One result of the brick tax was that the building of the canals, the early railways and many mills and factories was made a good deal more expensive. There was also an incentive to use stone whenever possible. The railways were great customers of the brickmakers. In 1821, before railway building began, the number of bricks charged with duty amounted to 913,231,000. In 1831 the total had risen to 1,153,048,581 and in 1840 to 1,725,628,333. It is not difficult to see why such immense numbers of bricks were needed. As one authority put it: 'A common turnpike road bridge over a railway requires for its construction, in round numbers, 300,000 bricks; and the lining of a railway tunnel of ordinary dimensions consumes about 8,000 for every yard in length, or in round numbers about 14,000,000 per mile.'[3]

In abandoning the tax on bricks, the Government was making a sacrifice of much the same order as the abolition of tobacco duty would involve today. In the year before the duty was repealed, a charge was made on 1800 million bricks. In 1854 the total was approximately 2000 million, of which about 130 million were made in the brickfields in and around Manchester and a similar number by the London brickmakers.

Clays suitable for brickmaking are found in many parts of the British Isles. They range from soft and plastic surface deposits, to hard mudstones, shales, marls and even some of the softer varieties of slate. Clay with good plasticity is better for hand moulding, but the machinery which is now available for crushing and grinding allows good bricks to be produced from the harder materials. The essential requirements are that after being ground and tempered with water, the clays and shales should be capable of taking a good shape, by moulding, extrusion or pressure, and that the shape should be retained without too much shrinkage, warping or cracking when the bricks are dried and fired.

The colours of most bricks are due mainly to the presence of iron oxides in the clay. Colours can be considerably modified by varying the amount of air admitted to the kiln during the later stages of firing and also by varying the temperature of firing. Under modern conditions this can be achieved reliably and predictably, but with the old type of clamp or kiln, when firing was controlled by rule of thumb and by individual expertise, the range of colours within a single batch and from batch to batch could be very wide. Many of the older brick buildings owe their pleasant texture and shade patterning to the brickmaker's inability to forecast exactly how his bricks were going to turn out. Some, inevitably, would be harder and darker than others.

Until the middle of the nineteenth century manufacture was a slow process and was mostly carried out near the site where the bricks were required. The clay was dug in the autumn and allowed to weather during the winter months. In the spring it was spread out, sprinkled with water and trodden into a pliable mass. The bricks were then moulded, air-dried under rough shelters and then fired in clamps or updraught kilns. The burning of bricks in clamps was often done near the building under construction. A foundation layer of burnt bricks was laid on a level piece of ground, to provide an insulation from rising damp. A layer of slack-coal or breeze was spread over the foundation. The 'green' bricks were stacked above it, burnt bricks and earth were laid over the top and the stack was then set on fire and allowed to burn itself out, a process which often took several weeks.

The updraught kilns allowed higher and more uniform temperatures to be obtained than in the clamp. The bricks became partly vitrified and, as a result, more durable. These kilns consisted of two chambers, one above the other. The fire was in the lower chamber and the bricks or tiles were fired in the upper chamber. Remains of this type of kiln exist all over the country, but, more frequently the only obvious evidence of early brickworks is provided by the old clay-pits, which often contain a dense growth of trees and bushes. Names like Brickyard Plantation, Brick-kiln Plantation, Brickyard Spinney or Brick-kiln Covert are clues to a vanished brickworks. So, too, are place-names such as Brickyard Lane and Brickyard Cottages.

Until the middle of the last century brick moulding was done by hand, but in 1741 William Bailey introduced his method of compacting the clay by means of rollers and in 1798 Francis Farquharson obtained the same result by pressing the clay under a heavy weight. The process known as wire cutting, in which a slab of clay was cut into bricks by dragging a wire through it, was invented by William Irving in 1841. The first extruding machine in Europe is reputed to have been made and used in Bridgwater in 1875. This machine continued in use, with no significant modification, until 1919. It was extremely simple; extrusion was carried out by means of a shaft which pushed the mass of clay between knives placed at right angles to each other.

Until the 1860s all kilns were of the type known as intermittent, that is, kilns which worked to a cycle of fill–fire–cool–empty. Kilns of this type are still used to make the more expensive kinds of facing and engineering bricks, but nowadays the great majority of building bricks are burnt in some form of continuous kiln. The pioneer in this was a German engineer, Friedrich Hoffmann. He designed his first continuous kiln in 1856 and patented it in 1858. It was circular and the fire was moved from one kiln opening to the next in turn. Hoffmann developed a continuous long-chamber kiln from this and built the first such kiln at Konstanz, in South Germany, in 1864. The continuous kiln consists essentially of a series of connected chambers in a circular or rectangular pattern, allowing the fire to be led gradually and progressively round the whole circuit. Burnt bricks are taken

out and green bricks placed in the chambers which at that moment
are furthest away from the fire. Kilns working on this principle use
much less fuel than intermittent kilns, partly because the fuel is
dropped in through feed-holes in the roof and burns actually among
the bricks and partly because much of the heat given up by the burnt
bricks as they cool is recirculated to dry and warm the newly set
green bricks and to heat the air passing to the fires. The difference in
efficiency is considerable. An intermittent kiln needs about a ton of
good coal for each 1000 bricks it produces, but a continuous kiln uses
only 3 to 5 cwt of slack in order to burn the same number.

As late as 1900, however, the great majority of bricks were burnt
in a type of intermittent kiln known as a Scotch kiln. This was a
large chamber, open at the top, with a series of fire holes down each
side opposite one another. The air-dried bricks were piled into these
kilns in such a way that flues were left connecting the fire holes and
that the fire could pass between and around the bricks from bottom
to top. A layer of old burnt bricks was then spread over the top, the
ends of the kiln were bricked up and roughly plastered over with clay
and fires were lit in the fire holes. When the burning process was
completed, the kiln was allowed to cool and the bricks taken out.
With this method of manufacture the shade of the bricks varied a
great deal in colour, those nearest the fire holes being the darkest in
colour. The harder burnt, darker bricks had also shrunk more, the
difference in size in the case of unpressed handmade bricks being considerable. The bricks from each chimney were roughly sorted, to
give the purchaser reasonably consistent lots.

Another type of intermittent kiln occasionally found during the
second half of the nineteenth century was the vaulted or domed kiln.
This was rectangular, with an inner and an outer shell, and had
about ten fire holes along each side of the outer shell. The heat rose
between the inner and outer walls, passed downwards through the
bricks to a perforated floor, on which the bricks were stacked, and
then through an air duct leading to a chimney.

A revolution in brickmaking took place at the end of the nineteenth century, when the manufacture of bricks from the Lower
Oxford Clay was begun at Fletton, near Peterborough. It was found
that the shale-like Fletton clay, which contained 18 to 20 per cent
moisture, could be pressed into a brick which could be fired immediately, without any previous drying. An equally important advantage

was that this clay contains about 10 per cent of carbonaceous material, which can be made to produce sufficient heat during firing to reduce the amount of coal required to something like a third of what has to be used with other clays.

The success of the new highly mechanised methods pioneered at Fletton persuaded other firms within the Oxford Clay area to adopt the Fletton process. The Forder works at Pulinge, now known as Stewartby, were producing Flettons in 1897. During the 1920s many of the smaller firms ran into financial difficulties and the three large companies now operating here came into being as a result of mergers and takeovers. The Marston Valley Brick Company built its Lidlington Works in 1929. After a series of amalgamations the Forder Company was absorbed into a much larger concern, which, in 1936, took the name of the London Brick Company, Eastwoods started production in 1938 at Kempston Hardwick. In 1962 they were taken over by Redland (Holdings) Limited and the works are now run by Redland (Flettons) Limited. These three companies, London Brick, Marston Valley Brick and Redland (Flettons) now produce, at their various works, not all of them in this area, considerably more than half of all the bricks used in Britain. The London Brick Company are the largest brickmakers in the world.

Until the 1930s only a common brick was produced in the Fletton area. It was the brick mainly used for the great expansion of London during the first forty years of the present century. After the new groups were formed, however, large quantities of faced bricks, too, were made. Despite relatively high transport costs the mechanisation and scale of production in the Fletton area, coupled with the exceptionally low fuel bills, made it possible for bricks from the Bedford, Peterborough and north Buckinghamshire areas to compete over most of Britain with the bricks made in local yards. It was this, more than any other single factor, which caused so many small brickworks to close down during the 1920s and 1930s and again, in a second wave, during the 1940s and 1950s.

Stewartby village, which adjoins Stewartby works, owes its existence entirely to the brick industry. It was named after the Chairman of what later became the London Brick Company, Sir P. Malcolm Stewart, and a former Chairman, Sir Hailey Stewart. The first houses were built in 1926 and there are now about 1000 people in this model village, living in 358 houses and bungalows.

Within the Bedfordshire brickfield the 111 chimneys dominate the landscape, in an area which is mainly flat and treeless. The chimneys are in six groups, the largest being at Stewartby, with thirty-two, and the smallest at Elslow, with five. They range in height from 100 to 300 feet. The trend is towards taller chimneys, as the most effective way of dealing with the serious pollution problem—the waste gases contain fluorine compounds and sulphur oxides, which kill trees and are dangerous to cattle. The brick industry has injured the landscape in another way: its vast pits have made thousands of acres derelict. This particular problem, however, is on the way to being solved. Some of the pits are to be filled with refuse from the London area—each acre takes about 30,000 tons of rubbish—and it is planned to use others for various kinds of water sports.

It is possible that the peak of brick production was reached in 1965 —the highest output so far—and that the industry now faces a steady and permanent decline. Compared with other wall-building components, a brick is very small and laying bricks demands a lot of what is now expensive labour. The higher-priced houses will probably continue to use bricks for some time to come, but these are just as likely to be supplied by small brickyards, specialising in high quality facing bricks, as by the giant firms in Bedfordshire. For most housing purposes, bricks and bricklayers are in the process of pricing themselves out of the market. In this situation, somewhat paradoxically, the cheap mass-produced bricks may be more vulnerable than the expensive handmade variety.

Although machine-made bricks have largely superseded hand-moulding, high quality facing bricks and certain special bricks are still hand-moulded. For handmoulding, clay of a good quality is required, made up rather softer than for wire-cut bricks. The moulder throws a lump of clay into the mould and packs its tightly into each corner, using a mallet or, nowadays, a pneumatic hammer. The surplus clay is cut off the top of the mould and the brick is turned out on to a rack or pallet. Handmade bricks have a special texture which cannot be produced on a machine and are always in demand for this reason.

Apart from handmoulding, four methods are used nowadays for making bricks:

(*a*) the wire process, for plastic clays;

(b) the stiff plastic process, mainly for colliery shales and for certain other clays and shales which do not easily develop a high degree of plasticity;

(c) the semi-dry press process, for the manufacture of bricks from the Oxford clays and from a number of other shales and clays with a low plasticity;

(d) the soft-mud or slop-moulded process, for making stock-bricks and multicoloured bricks.

The term 'stock-brick' is somewhat misleading. In south-east England 'stock-brick' has generally meant a brick made on a stock, a piece of wood fixed to a handmoulder's bench which holds the wooden mould into which the clay is thrown. The name 'stock-brick' is still used in the south-east to describe machinemade bricks which are similar in appearance to the old handmade stock. In other parts of the country a 'stock-brick' has quite a different meaning, the stock or usual brick made in the local yard, and it may be a wirecut or pressed brick according to the district. A 'London-stock' has a definite meaning. It is the familiar rough-textured yellow brick of which much of central London and the inner suburbs is built. London stock-bricks are not made from London clay, but from deposits of clay and chalk which occur in Kent and Essex, close to the banks of the Thames.

Until recently, brick- and tile-making were often combined in the same works, where the clay was suitable for both purposes. The flat clay tile has changed very little over the past 500 years. The original measurements, $10\frac{1}{2}$ by $6\frac{1}{2}$ by $\frac{1}{2}$ inches, have proved satisfactory and convenient.

The curved pantile was introduced into England during the seventeenth century. It became commonly used in the eastern and northern counties, where many tiles of this type were imported from Holland and Belgium. The manufacture of pantiles was well established in East Anglia by the end of the eighteenth century. They were mostly red in colour and unglazed, but some were given a black vitreous finish. The tiles were usually hand-moulded, but machine pressing was gradually introduced from the middle of the nineteenth century onwards. Firing was carried out in kilns very similar to those used for firing bricks.

The tile trade was conservative in its methods and usually short of capital, so that the units of production tended to remain small

9 Turning a Bath stone baluster on a lathe at Box, Wiltshire

10 A mason working on Bath stone tracery for restoration of Cheltenham College

11 Brick-making clay heaped behind the moulding shed at Puriton, Somerset. To obtain uniform consistency, which is essential during drying and firing, the stack was left to consolidate for six months to a year before use

12 Old King's Dyke Brick Works, Whittlesey, Peterborough

13 Brick-making by hand. Removing the green bricks for stacking and drying, Woodham Walter, Essex

14 Outdoor tile-drying racks, Puriton, Somerset. When these were in use, clay was dug in the winter and tiles made when there was no risk of frost

15 Split moulds for double Roman ridge tiles. When the works was in full production 60–70 hand moulders were employed at Puriton, making over 14,000 tiles a day

16 Ridge tile cutting table. In the background are stacked portable tile racks

Figure 4   Hatcher Beneden tile machine, 1844

throughout the nineteenth century and well into the twentieth. There were, however, some cases of enterprise. In 1899, to increase its range of products and to lower the cost of roofing tiles, the Somerset Trading Company patented and manufactured the Somerset interlocking tile, which subsequently became very popular. A big export trade was built up and new plant was designed and installed at Chilton Trinity. The industry came to a standstill during the 1914–18 war and afterwards further mechanisation and improvement was delayed because ample labour was available to continue with obsolete methods of manufacture. During the later 1920s and the 1930s, however, with the help of re-equipment and new investment, the Bridgwater tile industry settled down to a fairly buoyant period of mass-production. An average of 5 million tiles were made each year until 1939, when war once again brought production to a stop. After the war the output of tiles never reached its prewar figure. In 1960 it was only half that of the highest annual production prior to 1939. The two main reasons for this decline, typical of most of the smaller centres of roofing-tile manufacture, were, on the one hand, a completely inadequate investment to provide for modernising plant and on the other serious competition from the considerably cheaper concrete tiles.

Tiles, like bricks, may be in the process of changing from a necessity to a luxury. Advances in engineering and construction methods are leading towards larger building components, but the roofing tile is at present supplied in small units, suitable for yesterday's techniques and wages. If tiled roofs are to survive, the answer may lie either in prefabricated and pretiled roof structures, or in larger tile units, possibly extruded.

It is interesting to see how the materials available for roofing have dictated the pitch of the roof. With the exception of slates and thatch, roofing materials were, until recently, uncertain in size and shape, and so it was necessary to pitch the roof steeply in order to run the water off as quickly as possible. The traditional pitch of the Cotswold stone roof was 55°, simply because the stone was so irregular in size and shape. The same was true of clay tiles. The old Kent handmade tiles were often irregular, probably because of difficulties in the burning, that a builder would order a load of tiles and a load of hay and bed the tiles on the roof over the load of hay. Roofs more than a hundred years old have been found to be perfectly sound as long as the hay was left untouched. Once it was handled after this lapse of time, it fell into dust.

Slates were the first type of roofing material, apart from sheet lead or copper, that could be safely laid to low pitches. It was the adaptation of design to a new type of roofing that made the Georgian style of house possible, with a low-pitched roof almost concealed behind parapet walls. Slates had certain disadvantages, however. If the nail holding a slate to the batten gave way, as it often did, the slate slid out of position. Unlike tiles, slates had no lengthwise camber and leaks were caused by water creeping back up the slate by capillary action. Concrete tiles, well compacted by heavy pressure, keep their shape and size completely during the drying out period and can be laid at pitches ranging from 15° to 80°.

A clay product much used by eighteenth- and nineteenth-century architects was terracotta. It was made by allowing the clay to weather for several months and then mixing it with what was known as grog. Grog was either sand or fired clay ground to a powder. By including it in the mix, the shrinkage during firing was reduced from the 15 per cent which is normal in brick or tile making to something like 8 per cent. The plastic material was then moulded, often into elaborate shapes, and then fired once, if the product was to be left unglazed, and twice for faience or glazed terracotta, the glaze being applied before the second firing. In the manufacture of faience, the body was fired at a high temperature and the body plus glaze at a low temperature.

The art of terracotta reached England from Italy. Henry VIII commissioned Italian craftsmen to make terracotta ornaments for his own palace at Hampton Court and for other great houses of the period, including Layer Marney in Essex. For some unexplained reason, English craftsmen did not take to this new skill and it remained a continental speciality until the eighteenth century. In 1722 Richard Holt and Thomas Ripley set up a factory in Lambeth to make terracotta. The business continued until the 1750s and then, in 1767, the premises, which had remained derelict for some years, were taken over by George and Eleanor Coade, who began to make a high quality type of terracotta, known eventually as Coade Stone. This was fired at a fairly high temperature, about 1100°C and seems to have included a flux of some kind, probably felspar or marl. The resulting product was very hard and weather-resistant. It has stood up excellently to the London atmosphere.

During the nineteenth century, Doultons of Lambeth made some very good decorative panels in terracotta. One of them, by George Tinworth, a friend of Ruskin, is in the reredos of York Minster.

There is a great deal of terracotta still to be seen in large cities. In London many surviving Victorian buildings include quantities of it, especially as ornaments and window surrounds. One of the most impressive of these monuments of terracotta is the Natural History Museum in South Kensington. Another is Doulton's old office and studio building, still standing at the corner of Lambeth High Street. Unfortunately, much of the terracotta produced during the nineteenth century was carelessly fired, at too low a temperature. It deteriorated fast, and architects became understandably wary of using it. Coade Stone, on the other hand, has proved practically indestructible. There is a good example of its superiority over ordinary terracotta in the gateway to Syon House, Brentford, built by Robert Adam. The original ornamental pillars, moulded in terracotta, did not wear well and early in the nineteenth century several sections were replaced by Coade Stone, which remains as sharp as the day it was installed.

Wherever terracotta on a late eighteenth- or early nineteenth-century building appears to be exceptionally well preserved, there is a strong probability that it came from the Coade works. The same is true of terracotta garden ornaments. A long list of known surviving examples of Coade Stone is included in Rubert Guinness's *Dictionary of British Sculptors* (1968)[4]. The most famous of them is undoubtedly the large lion, which was originally on top of the Lion Brewery on the South Bank. At the time of the Festival of Britain it was given a place of honour by the steps leading up to Waterloo Station and it now crouches, rather less prominently and unfortunately painted white, at the County Hall end of Westminster Bridge.

The growing Victorian concern with hygiene and public health provided manufacturers of stoneware and what came to be called sanitary pipeware with remarkable opportunities. One of the best known of these firms was Doultons of Lambeth, established in 1815.[5] During the first sixty years of its existence this company made chiefly salt-glazed stoneware and, in the form of drainpipes and conduits, this still represents an important part of the company's output today. Stoneware is fired at not less than 1200°C. During the firing process common salt is thrown or sprayed into the kiln As it vaporises, the sodium combines with the clay to form a very hard glaze and the chlorine passes off as vapour. Stoneware bottles, jars and pots had been made in Lambeth since the late seventeenth century, and for a few years Doultons confined themselves to this type of product. In the mid 1820s, however, they, like other Lambeth potters, began to make stoneware waterpipes.

Castiron waterpipes had been used at Versailles in the late seventeenth century, but wooden mains were still normal in Britain in 1810. They were gradually replaced by castiron, as a result of growing anxiety about polluted water supplies, but for some time stoneware pipes were used by a number of the water companies. The major expansion of the Doulton factory, however, was based on its development work in the fields of acid-resistant stoneware for the chemical industry and of drainpipes. Doulton's pioneered the use of stoneware drainpipes. They were desperately needed. Between 1750 and 1850 the number of town dwellers in England rose from two to ten million. The great majority of them got their water from wells, springs and rivers which had been polluted by overflowing cesspools and defective drains and sewers. Epidemics of typhoid, typhus, cholera and dysentery were frequent and inevitable.[6] In 1861 the Prince Consort himself died of typhoid fever, caused by the drains at Windsor Castle.

BRICKS AND TILES

Sir Edwin Chadwick, the great advocate of public health measures, suggested to Henry Doulton that he should experiment with the manufacture of glazed stoneware pipes for sewers and house drains. To start with the sockets for the pipes were made separately and attached to the extruded tubes by hand. A satisfactory press, which extruded pipes and sockets in one piece, was patented in 1848, the year of the Public Health Act. The demand for glazed drainage pipes grew so fast that Doulton's set up additional pipe factories at St Helens and Dudley. In 1852 Henry Doulton persuaded the sixteen other firms making stoneware pipes in London to join him in forming the London Potters' Association, to control quality and dimensions. One of their first acts was to agree to manufacture pipes to certain standard thicknesses.

Diameter	3 in.	4 in.	6 in.	8 in.	9 in.	10 in.
Thickness	$\frac{1}{2}$ in.	$\frac{1}{2}$ in.	$\frac{5}{8}$ in.	$\frac{11}{16}$ in.	$\frac{3}{4}$ in.	$\frac{7}{8}$ in.
Diameter	12 in.	15 in.	18 in.			
Thickness	1 in.	$1\frac{1}{4}$ in.	$1\frac{1}{2}$ in.			

These rations have changed very little since they were established.

Doulton's were also prominent in improving and marketing sanitary fittings. Until the middle of the nineteenth century neither baths nor water closets were at all common in the homes of the wealthy, and they were non-existent any lower in the social scale. George IV had a marble bath at Brighton Pavilion, but when Queen Victoria inherited it on her accession to the throne in 1837 she had it sawn up to make mantlepieces for Buckingham Palace, where there was no bath at all until Albert installed one in his bedroom twenty years later.

Harington's invention of the water closet late in the sixteenth century is well known, but little came of it until Joseph Bramah took out his patent for an effective valve closet in 1778. The early water closets were cast in lead or carved in marble or stone, but by the beginning of the nineteenth century they were being made of glazed pottery and the market for them had spread to the middle classes. Stoneware closets with conical-shaped pans and separate traps were sold by Doulton's in 1817 at 3 shillings each. By 1848 they were making up to 200 a week.

In 1859 Doulton designed and manufactured the first glazed ceramic kitchen sink. It was easily cleaned and an immense improvement on the old stone sinks, but for some unexplained reason the

British refused to buy them. Doulton's persevered, and fortunately found a ready market in France. By the 1880s, the public attitude had changed in England and the old stone sinks gradually began to give way to the enamelled fireclay sinks and basins now in use.

Another well-known company to specialise in sanitary pottery was Jennings South Western Pottery at Parkstone in Dorset, founded in 1856. Jenning's original pottery was in Lambeth. He held many patents and was the chief sanitary engineer for the Great Exhibition in 1851. Soon after the outbreak of the Crimean War he manufactured sanitary fittings for the British hospitals at Varna and Scutari, where they were fixed by a staff of his own workmen from the Lambeth works. In the early 1930s the Jennings Pottery installed the first continuous salt-glazing pipe-producing tunnel to be built in Britain. This produced large quantities of sanitary pipeware, much of it for export, until the outbreak of war in 1939, when the plant was closed.

CHAPTER FOUR

Lime, Cement, Plaster and Concrete

The earliest cements, as used by the Egyptians to cover rough brick and stone-work and prepare it for painting, were made from gypsum, a form of calcium sulphate.[1] This material can be dehydrated at fairly low temperatures, but it is soluble in water and consequently unsuitable for outside use in countries which, like England but unlike Egypt, have a good deal of rain. It is, however, a perfectly good material, even in wet climates, for indoor use. Gypsum plaster was introduced into England from France—hence the name 'plaster of Paris'—in the thirteenth century, mainly for providing the walls and ceilings of important houses and public buildings with a smooth, hard finish, sometimes with moulded ornamentation. Until about 1900 plaster of Paris remained comparatively expensive in England and consequently most of the plaster used for indoor finishes was made of a mixture of lime and sand, with a little ox or cow hair added to it in order to bind the plaster together and stop it from cracking. The same type of plaster was used on the outside of buildings in England from the sixteenth century onwards. It was known as pargetting or parging. It is found, especially in Essex and Suffolk, on timber-framed buildings. The surface of the plaster was often finished with rough-cast or pebble-dash of various kinds, but in East Anglia it was patterned by using pointed combs and sticks. A number of beautiful examples of this type of work can be seen at Thaxted and Lavenham.

When old houses are being pulled down or renovated, the materials and techniques used for plastering in previous centuries can easily be noticed. They range from the bottom layer of clay and chopped straw mixture spread over a wattle base in cottages to the much finer lime plasters used in eighteenth- and nineteenth-century houses, over a screen of split laths.

During the fifteenth and sixteenth centuries the Italians began to study Roman methods of plastering and to attempt to copy them. They used a *stucco duro*, a mixture of old air-slaked lime and marble dust, sometimes with a little gypsum added to help it to set. Henry VIII employed Italian workmen for the stucco decorations in his new palace of Nonsuch, which was demolished in 1670. Excavations carried out on the site during the 1950s revealed pieces of the stucco work, still in excellent condition after being exposed to rain and frost for more than a century.[2] The craft of lime stucco was soon learnt by English workmen. Old Hardwick Hall (1590–97) contains English stucco work of good quality.

Until the seventeenth century modelling in plaster was not elaborate, except in the case of ceiling pendants, but Inigo Jones, Wren and Grinling Gibbons introduced much bolder concepts, with domes, cornices and deep undercutting. The fruit and flowers used by Gibbons included strips of lead, wires and twigs in the plaster composition. Much of this ornamentation was cast in small pieces and assembled on the site. The stucco mixture used in England included a wide range of exotic substances, all intended to improve the adhesive qualities of the plaster. One authority has identified 'rye dough, barley water, hog's lard, bullock's blood, cow dung, wort and eggs, wort and beer, milk, gluten, buttermilk, cheese, curdled milk, saponified beeswax, fig and other fruit and vegetable juices'.[3]

In the middle of the eighteenth century another group of stucco mixtures became popular with architects. They were known as 'oil mastics' or 'oleaginous cements'. Two of them, one patented by David Wark in 1765, and the other by Liandet in 1773, were bought by the Adam brothers, who marketed them as 'Adams Patent Stucco', later known as 'Adams Cement'. It was used on the fronts of buildings in Portland Place, Hanover Square and Bedford Square, but it proved unsuitable for exteriors and the Adams lost a good deal of money as a result. Other compositions were patented by Christopher Dihl (1815 and 1816) and by Hamelin (1817). Dihl's cement contained linseed oil, lead oxide, china clay and ground brick, with turpentine as a thinner. John Nash used it for the stucco and ornamental work at Carlton House Terrace (1827–33) and for the ornaments at Regent's Park Terrace (1821–24). Hamelin mixed linseed oil, lead oxide, powdered limestone, brickdust and siliceous sand. His cement was used by Nash for the front of the United Services Club

LIME, CEMENT, PLASTER AND CONCRETE

(1828) and by Decimus Burton for the frieze of the Athenaeum Club (1829–30).

The plasterer's tools and basic skills changed very little during the eighteenth and nineteenth centuries. They remained much as Joseph Moxon described them in his *Mechanick Exercises* (1678), where he listed them as:

1. A *Lathing Hammer* being the same as before in Tyling, with which the laths are nailed on with its head and with its Edge they cut them to any length, and likewise cut off any part of a Quarter, or Joyst, that sticks further out than the rest.
2. A *Laying Trowel*, to lay the Lime and Hair withall upon the Laths, it being larger than a *Brick Trowel*, and fastned its handle in a different manner from the *Brick Trowel*.
3. A *Hawke*, made of wood about the bigness of a square Trencher, with a handle to hold it by, whereon the Lime and Hair being put, they take from it more or less as they please.
4. A *Setting Trowel*, being less than the *Laying Trowel*, with which they finish the Plastering when it is almost dry, either by Trowelling and brishing it over with fair *Water*, or else by laying a thin Coat of fine stuff made of clean lime, and mixt with Hair without any Sand, and setting it, that is to say, Trowelling and brishing it.
5. A small *Pointing Trowel*, to go into sharp Angles.
6. Brishes, of three sorts, viz. A *Stock Brish*, a *Round Brish*, and a *Pencil*. With these *Brishes*, they wet old walls before they mend them, and also brish over their new Plastering when they set, or finish it, and moreover white and size their Plastering with them. The *Pencil* or *Drawing Tool*, is used in blacking the bottoms, or lower ports of Rooms, &c.
7. *Floats*, made of Wood, with handles to them, which they sometimes use to float Seelings or Walls with, when they are minded to make their Plastering very streight and even, these *Floats* being some larger and some lesser, than the *Laying Trowels*: Likewise they use *Floats* made to fit to Mouldings, for the finishing of several sorts of Mouldings with finishing Morter to represent Stone, such as *Cornices, Facias, Archytraves*, &c. The finishing Morter to represent Stone, should be made of the strongest Lime and the sharpest Sand you can get, which

sand must be washed in a large Tub, very well, till no Scum or Filth arise in the Water, when you stir about, which sometimes will require to have Water 5 to 6 times, when the Sand is somewhat foul; and it requires a greater Proportion of Sand than the ordinary Morter, because it must be extreamly beaten, which will break all the knots of *Lime*, and by that means it will require more Sand.

8. *Straight Rules* of several lengths, to lay Quines streight by, and also to try whether the Plastering be laid true and streight, by applying the Rules to their Work.
9. A *Pale*, to hold *Water* or *Whitewash*, or *White* and *Size*.
10. Some use a *Budget* or *Pocket* to hang by their sides, to put their *Nails* in when they *hath*, and others Tuck and tye up their *Aprons*, and put the *Nails* therein.

During the eighteenth century many experiments were made to find ways of improving lime mortar. The traditional method of first burning the chalk or limestone and then mixing it with sand and water produced a mortar which hardened as the calcium hydroxide became converted to calcium carbonate. This was, however, a slow process, which often affected only the outside of the mortar layer. By adding some form of siliceous matter, such as volcanic ash or burnt clay, to lime mortar, a much more satisfactory product was obtained, with the whole mass of mortar becoming more resistant to rain or sea-water. The Greeks and Romans made extensive use of siliceous additions, or pozzolanas[4] to their mortars, and this is one of the main reasons why their buildings have survived for so long. As well as natural pozzalanic material the Romans added crushed bricks, tiles or pottery, with much the same beneficial result. In Britain this was the normal practice. Once mortars of this stronger type became generally used by the Romans it became possible to support buildings with much thinner walls and to construct arches and vaults.

Hydraulic (i.e. water-resistant) lime can also be obtained by burning limestone which contains a proportion of clay, a discovery which belongs to the second half of the eighteenth century. One of the pioneers in this field was John Smeaton, who visited Holland in 1754 and was impressed by the Dutch 'tarras mortar'—a mixture of pozzolanic earth and slaked lime—which was used in the construction of harbours and sea-defences. He experimented with different kinds of lime and discovered that well-burnt Aberthaw blue lias, which contained some clay, produced a cement which hardened satisfactorily. For the Eddystone lighthouse he eventually decided to use a mixture of Aberthaw limestone and pozzolana from Civita Vecchia, in Italy.

By the end of the eighteenth century the demand for reliable hydraulic cement had begun to rise rapidly. There were two main reasons for this. The first was the London Building Act of 1774, which encouraged the use of stucco as a facing for buildings; the second was the greatly increased scale of the civil engineering works required for the development of canals, harbours and bridges. This demand was made even more pressing by the railway building of the 1840s. It was a demand which a succession of inventors did everything possible to meet, and by 1850 there were three types of cement available for making a mortar or concrete which would set in the absence of air, or in a damp atmosphere.

The first of these was made by burning stone which contained a suitable mixture of lime, alumina and silica. A number of patents for these 'natural' hydraulic cements were taken out between 1790 and 1830. They included James Parker's (1796) for a 'Roman' cement, made from septaria or nodules of argillaceous limestone which lay in large quantities along the northern shore of the Thames estuary, especially along the coast of the Isle of Sheppey. In his patent, Parker described the process as follows:

> 'The stones of clay or noddles of clay are first broken into small fragments, then burnt in a kiln, or furnace (as lime is commonly burned) with a heat nearly sufficient to virtify them, then reduced to powder by any mechanical or other operation, and the powder so obtained is the basis of the cement.'

Parker's patent lapsed in 1810, and after that septaria from the Harwich area were increasingly used, so much so that more than a million tons were taken from the Harwich foreshore between 1812 and 1825, when the Government prohibited any digging closer than 50 feet from the base of the cliffs. After that as many as 300 boats, each with a crew of three or four men, were employed dredging these 'cement-stones' from the sea-bed.

In the trade, the misleading term 'Roman cement' came to mean cement made by burning a mixture of the cheaper Harwich stones with a small proportion of Sheppey stones. The best 'Roman cement' contained mainly Sheppey stones, but another of equal quality, known variously as 'Atkinson's', 'Mulgrave', 'Whitby' or 'Yorkshire' came from near Whitby. Good quality cement also came from the Isle of Wight, Weymouth Bay and Lyme Regis. Cement from this area was known as 'Medina' cement.

Telford used Parker's cement in the construction of Chirk Viaduct (1796–1801), which carries the Ellesmere Canal across the River Ceiriog. The viaduct was made watertight by backing the masonry with hard-baked bricks laid in Parker's cement. Another customer was Marc Isambard Brunel, who ordered it for the Wapping-Rotherhithe tunnel (1825–43).

The second group, the 'artificial' or proprietary cements, were made by mixing limestone or chalk with clay or shale in the right proportions, discovered and controlled empirically, and then burning the mixture at a temperature of between 1100 and 1300°C. The pioneer here seems to have been a Frenchman, Baron Louis Bernard Guyton de Morveau, who, in 1774, calcined a mixture of 90 per cent chalk, 6 per cent clay and 4 per cent manganese dioxide and then ground the product to a fine powder. During the 1820s Sir Charles Pasley, who commanded the School of Military Engineering at Chatham, carried out many experiments, involving grinding a burnt mixture of chalk and clay, in order to produce a synthetic hydraulic cement, with considerable success. Joseph Aspdin's so-called Portland cement, patented in 1824, should probably be put in this group, although in his patent no mention is made of the essential feature of true Portland cement, burning at a temperature sufficiently high to produce partial vitrification.

The patent shows both Aspdin's method and the small scale of his operations at this time:

> 'I take a specific quantity of limestones such as that generally used for making or repairing roads, and I take it from the roads after it is reduced to a puddle or powder; but if I cannot procure a sufficient quantity of the above from the roads, I obtain the limestone itself, and I cause the puddle or powder, or the limestone, as the case may be to be calcined. I then take a specific quantity of argillaceous earth of clay, and mix them with water to a state approach-

ing impalpability, either by manual labour or machinery. After this proceeding I put the above mixture into a slip pan for evaporation, either by the heat of the sun, or by submitting it to the action of fire or steam conveyed in flues or pipes under or near the pan until the water is entirely evaporated. Then I break the said mixture into suitable lumps and calcine them in a furnace similar to the lime kiln till the carbonic acid is entirely expelled. The mixture so calcined is to be ground, beat or rolled to a fine powder.'

When Aspdin took out his patent, he was in business with William Beverley as 'Patent Portland cement manufacturers' at Briggate, Leeds, and Kirkgate, Wakefield. It is possible that he made Portland cement accidentally, by burning his raw material at a higher temperature than was customary. This may have happened because he used a glass furnace, instead of the normal lime kiln. However, whether or not Aspdin really produced or was the first to produce the material now known as Portland cement, there can be no doubt that, in his patent, he was the first to use the term 'Portland cement'. He chose the name, in all probability, because Portland stone had a high reputation for quality. It set a standard. Thirty years before Smeaton said that he wanted 'to make a cement that would equal the best merchantable Portland Stone in solidity and durability'.

In any case, by the 1850s the true Portland cements formed a third, distinct group. They consisted mainly of calcium silicates, produced by using a temperature of 1300–1400°C order to ensure as complete a reaction as possible between the lime and the silica. The chemical processes involved were not understood at all before the 1850s and for two decades after that manufacturing still contained a good deal of trial and error, at least in England. The first reliable Portland cement was produced in 1845 by I. C. Johnson, at Swanscombe, in Kent. Large quantities were exported from Swanscombe for use in the construction of the new harbour works at Cherbourg (1858). Johnson subsequently opened a second works at Gateshead. The new Portland cement works had to be situated close to easily available sources of chalk or clay. This explains the concentration of works in the Thames Basin, where the North Downs provided ample supplies of chalk and London clay, and the mud deposits of the Thames and Medway were near at hand. The cement industry established itself in Kent during the second half of the eighteenth century and this area has continued to be of great importance ever since. In addition to the advantage of having chalk and clay close by, the North Kent cement works were well placed for shipping in coal by sea and for transporting the cement to London—the main market—in river barges. Gateshead had similar advantages.

The remains of early lime-kilns are plentifully scattered over Britain in the chalk and limestone areas, but there is little surviving evidence of the early Portland cement-kilns, although the two types were basically very similar. The lime-kilns were usually square-sectioned masonry structures, with the interior of the kiln in the shape of a truncated milk bottle. They were frequently built into a hillside, so that fuel and limestone could be tipped in from above and the burnt material removed through a draw-hole at the bottom. There are a number of such kilns, dating from the later eighteenth century, along the North Devon coast from Glenthorne to Hartland. Particularly well preserved specimens can be seen at Haddon's Mouth, Lee Bay and Woody Bay and on the promenade at Lynmouth a group of old lime-kilns has been converted into a shelter for holidaymakers. Another series of Devonshire kilns, in a ruinous condition, is along the Tamar, between Gunnislake and Plymouth. On the island of Lindisfarne, in Northumberland, there is a battery of lime-kilns in a good state of preservation, with a track linking the kilns to the quarry on one side and to a jetty on the other. The site of the new open-air museum at Dudley, in Staffordshire, includes a group of large early nineteenth century lime-kilns, built here in order to take advantage of the canal running close by.

One interesting limeworks, near Merstham, in Surrey, has been recently revealed by a team of archaeologists working under the direction of Eric S. Wood. The site is close to the southern end of the Merstham railway tunnel and the limeworks was set up by the contractors, Jolliffe and Banks. Two circles were excavated by Mr Wood and provided evidence that they had been used for mixing mortar to line the first Merstham tunnel.

The kilns which were at first used to produce Portland cement were like the traditional lime-kilns. They were operated on an intermittent basis. Wood faggots, coal and coke were put on the grate and set on fire, and then the kiln was filled with alternate layers of limestone or cement stone and coke. When the mass had burnt itself out, the calcined lime or cement was drawn out at the bottom of the kiln. It was an expensive process, because the kiln cooled down while it was being reloaded and a considerable quantity of fuel was needed to heat it up again. Kilns of this type used for lime-burning used about $4\frac{1}{2}$ cwt of coal for each ton of lime produced. The chief difference between the lime-kiln and the Portland cement-kiln was that the cement-kiln was built considerably narrower at the open end, in order to conserve heat as much as possible and to induce a fiercer draught. To overcome these disadvantages, the Dietsch kiln was introduced from Germany in 1880. This kiln operated continuously. Firing took place only in the bottom third of the kiln, which was lined with refractory bricks on account of the higher temperatures which were possible. The cement clinker dropped into a compartment below the firing area, where it was air-cooled by a forced draught, blown in to increase the intensity of the heat above in the calcining chamber.

A rotary kiln was patented by Thomas Russell Crompton in 1877, but it was unsatisfactory. Improved versions were patented by Frederick Ransome (1885) and Frederick Stokes (1886). These allowed the raw materials to be pumped into the kiln as a wet slurry, without the need for previous drying. The kiln revolved in a tilted position, with the firing area at the lower end. Ransome's kiln was installed at Arlesey in the late 1880s. By modern standards it was very small, being only 25 ft long and 5 ft in diameter. The rotary kiln was not commercially successful for some years, although the basic principle was obviously sound. In 1900, however, since the demand for cement was rising so fast that some form of large-scale, continuous production was essential, the newly formed Associated Portland Cement Manufacturers' Association bought the rights to an improved American version of Crompton's kiln and built new plant of this type on their Thames-side site at Northfleet.

After the original inventions had been made, the most important development work was done in Germany, largely as a result of scientific control of the raw materials, processing and testing.[5] By 1875 the better German cements were reaching compression strengths 80 per cent higher than in 1860, and tests made in 1885 showed a further increase of 60 per cent compared with 1875. It was only with the availability of the greatly improved cements of the 1880s that reinforced concrete construction became practicable, although the idea had been known for many years.[6] The word 'concrete', like 'cement' has to be handled with some care in any historical study. The Romans used brick and stone grouted with mortar for foundations and for the core of walls and the medieval churches and cathedrals contain masses of rubble and mortar in their walls and pillars. This is not concrete in the modern sense. The material was not mixed before laying and there was no attempt to use calculated proportions of lime or cement, sand and aggregate.

Between 1770 and 1820 there are a number of recorded instances of the use of crude forms of concrete in the foundations of large structures. In 1770, George Dance, 'having to sink the principal foundations of Newgate Prison to a depth of 40 ft in consequence of their site being partly on the ancient ditch of London Wall, threw into the bog cartloads of whole and broken brick and cartloads of mortar in the proportion of 1 to 4'.[7] Small pieces of Kentish ragstone, grouted with a very liquid mortar, were used as a filler between the heads of the piles on which Waterloo Bridge was built in 1811 and Sir Robert Smirke employed the grouting method for the Penitentiary on Millbank (1816) and the foundations of the General Post Office in St Martin-le-Grand (1825–29, demolished 1912–13). For the Penitentiary he laid 'a stratum of grouted gravel', that is, a concrete raft, as foundations. The mixture consisted of 1 part lime, 5–7 parts clean gravel and water. As each layer was added, labourers pounded it down with their feet, wearing what were known as 'puddling boots'. Before the late 1820s Smirke never used the word 'concrete', and what he laid as foundations was not what we would call concrete nowadays. It was not, in fact, until the late 1830s that 'concrete' was generally understood in its modern sense—cement, aggregate and water, thoroughly mixed together before being in position. Although not a true pioneer—material similar to concrete had been used for the concrete foundations of Toulon Harbour as early as 1748 and for the Avant Port at Cherbourg in 1804—Smirke is an important figure in the development of concrete technology, mainly because his use of 'grouted gravel' in foundations allowed large buildings to be successfully constructed on difficult sites.

In the essay, *The Nature and Properties of Concrete*, for which he received a prize from the Royal Institute of British Architects in 1836, George Godwin gives the impression that he believed 'concrete' to be a modern word, or, at least, to have changed its meaning

17 A traditional and still fashionable building material. Thatching at Sopley, Hampshire

18 Stone tiled roofs, Bradford-on-Avon, Wiltshire

19 The remains of a battery of Aspdin cement kilns which originally stood at Northfleet, Kent

20 Lime-stone kilns at Tipton Road, Dudley, built in 1842 with convenient canal access. The water submerging the bottom part of the kilns is overflow from the adjacent sewage treatment plant

21 Ransome's rotary kiln at Arlesey, Bedfordshire, 1887. One of the earliest kilns of this type to be installed in Britain

22 Cement works at Burham, near Rochester, Kent, from a poster of 1874

23 The Iron Palace of King Eyambo, 1853

24 Iron house for Châgres, Panama, commissioned by the Royal Mail Steam Packet Company, 1853

in recent years. 'The generic term "concrete",' he writes, 'can perhaps only date from that period when its use became general and frequent, probably not longer than fifteen or twenty years ago.' Even so, what he calls concrete does not seem at that time to have been used for anything other than foundations. A normal mixture, he records, was 1 part of lime to 4–12 parts of ballast, rubble or broken granite.

> 'They are sometimes mixed together, slaked as mortar, and thrown into the foundation from a certain height; sometimes the ballast is laid on the site of the intended erection, and the lime poured over it in the shape of grout; while at other times the spaces to be concreted are filled with water, and the lime and ballast having first been mixed in the proper proportions, are thrown into it dry.'

It is clear that Godwin, even at that date, did not consider it essential to mix the materials, including the water, together before laying the concrete, but ten years later this is known to have become the general practice.

Between about 1870 and 1939 speculative builders with large estates of houses to construct as cheaply as possible often used, for foundations and as a ground layer between the footings of the walls, concrete made from burnt ballast. This was made by mixing clay with coal dust and burning it in large heaps, close to the site where it was to be used. In the middle of these heaps, the clay was burnt to a hard clinker, which produced concrete of good quality, but much of the heap was inevitably underburnt and when it was mixed with cement and water it softened and became almost useless. Much of the cracking and dampness—some of it very serious—which occurred in the walls of houses built in the London area during the 1920s and 1930s was caused by the use of burnt ballast.

The first examples of the use of iron in conjunction with true concrete consisted of wrought-iron girders, joined by thin curved iron plates at the base and with the space above the plates and between the girders filled in with concrete. Sir William Fairbairn patented such a system in 1844 and in 1845 made use of it in an eight-storey sugar refinery in Manchester. The Fox and Barrett floors, much used for industrial buildings during the 1840s, had wrought iron joists, with the tops only bedded in concrete.

A good deal of experimental work with reinforced concrete was carried out in France in the 1840s and 1850s. In 1849 Joseph Monier made tubs for orange trees, with a mesh of iron rods embedded in the concrete. Later, from 1867 onwards, he took out a number of patents which showed an understanding of the stress resistant properties of iron and concrete when bonded together. Jean Louis Lambot had a provisional patent in 1855 for what he described as 'an Improved Building Material to be used as a substitute for wood', and said his method was to 'make this substitute of a network, or a parallel set of wires, or metallic bars or rods. imbedded or cemented together with hydraulics or other cementing matter, so as to form beams or planes of any suitable size'. A concrete boat demonstrating his meshsystem exhibited at the Paris Exhibition of 1855, but, in celebrating the Centenary of Reinforced Concrete in Paris in 1948, the French dated Lambot's invention back to 1848, when he is supposed to have floated a reinforced concrete boat on his lake.

On the most reliable evidence, however, the real pioneer of reinforced concrete as a structural material was an Englishman, W. B. Wilkinson, whose patent for reinforced concrete beams (no. 2293, 1854) was based on an awareness of the technical problems involved in constructing concrete beams. Wilkinson's fireproof floor beams were reinforced with lengths of old wire colliery ropes, frayed out at the ends in order to ensure close bonding with the concrete and correctly positioned within the beam to provide maximum strength. The concrete was very coarse. The patent describes it as composed of 'three parts of crushed hard-burnt bricks, passed through a riddle or 2 inch mesh, and two parts of hammer-broken stones or bricks, half broken to 2 inches in diameter and half to the size of a quarter brick, and mixed with Portland or other cement of good quality'. The only certain evidence of the use Wilkinson made of his patent was a cottage he built at Newcastle upon Tyne, probably in 1865. This cottage, the earliest reinforced concrete house in the world, was pulled down in 1954, but a careful record was made at the time.[8] The oldest surviving house built in reinforced concrete is probably that built by William E. Ward at Port Chester, New York (1873). Wilkinson was advertising concrete flooring in 1865. It was 'adopted by the War Office and used in practically every barracks and troop stable, as well as by Royalty, noblemen and landed gentlemen in their coach and hunting stables, farm buildings, kennels, etc.'[9] In

LIME, CEMENT, PLASTER AND CONCRETE

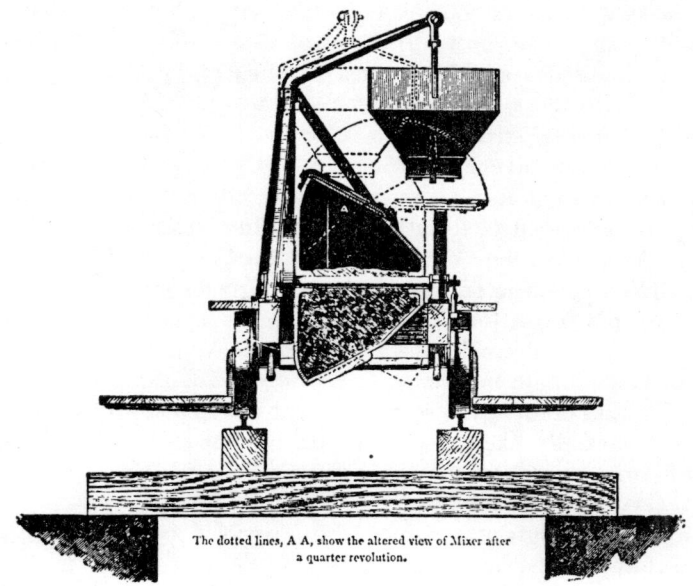

The dotted lines, A A, show the altered view of Mixer after a quarter revolution.

Figure 5   Early concrete mixer, built *c.* 1860. Two men were employed to fill the hopper and four to turn the handles

1883 he laid a concrete tennis court at Sandringham for the Prince of Wales.

A year after Wilkinson's patent, François Coignet patented his method of encasing iron joists in concrete, but the position of the iron, in the centre of the slab, indicates that he had little conception of the main principle of reinforced concrete. His concrete was, however, much more satisfactory than Wilkinson's. For the roof of his own house, built in 1853, before the patent was taken out, he used gravel, lime and cement, in the proportions of 5 to 1 to $1\frac{1}{2}$, with a 1 cm mesh and the whole mixture very well compacted.

It was not until the 1880s, however, that sufficiently strong and reliable cements were available to make reinforced concrete construction practical. Between 1880 and 1900 a number of able and enthusiastic research engineers and architects, mostly in Germany and France, were able to establish the characteristics of reinforced concrete and to work out calculations for structures using this material. One of the most important of them was François Hennebique, who discovered the nature of shearing stress in concrete (1880) and the way of counteracting it by introducing vertical J-shaped bars, called stirrups, into the ends of the beam to bond the upper and lower layers together. By 1900 several engineers and builders in Europe and America, notably Hennebique, Wayss and Ransome, developed techniques for resisting shear by bending the ends of the torsion bars upwards at an angle of 45°. Hennebique's first building constructed entirely of reinforced concrete—walls and roof, as well as frame—was the sugar refinery at St Ouen (1894–95). His most advanced work was the mill, Le Moulin Idéal, at Nort (1898). The monolithic frame of reinforced concrete embodied all the techniques of scientific reinforcement developed up to that time, in ways essentially like those in use today. The main innovations in this building were the use of thin precast slabs for the curtain walls and precast window mullions.

Since 1900 a high proportion of the world's leading architects—and, unfortunately, many of the worst as well—have frequently chosen reinforced concrete in preference to all other materials, largely because they feel that it allows them an exceptional degree of freedom to solve design problems in a fully satisfying and uncompromising way. The Swiss engineer and architect, Robert Maillart, is an excellent case in point. He has used concrete to build some of the most graceful and efficient bridges in the world, bridges, such as that over the Rhine at Tavarnasa (1905), which it is impossible to imagine carried out in any other material. Maillart's famous mushroom-slab construction, too, is inconceivable in anything else but reinforced concrete. The first example of this new technique is a warehouse in Zurich (1910), where the normal beams are eliminated and the floor slab itself takes over their static functions.

Reinforced concrete has also shown remarkable capacity for solving the problems of large-span roofs. Some ingenious structures of this type were built between 1910 and 1925. One of the best known was Max Bery's Centenary Hall in Breslau (1912–13), which was severely damaged during the 1939–45 war. In this building the central area of the assembly hall was roofed with concrete ribs over 200 feet in diameter. Eugène Freyssinet's two airship hangars at Orly (1916–24) are equally impressive. They are, in effect, barrel vaults constructed of a thin skin of concrete which has been pleated to give the necessary rigidity.

Of the outstanding early artists in reinforced concrete, the one with the longest career and widest range was Auguste Perret. Beginning with a small house in the rue Franklin, Paris, where the façade gains its effect by the contrast between the load-bearing frame and the infilling panels, he went on to design a garage for Renault (1905) in the rue de Ponthieu, Paris and the Théâtre des Champs-Elysées (1911). His industrial and technical buildings included the Esders Clothing Factory, Paris (1919), the Admiralty Research Laboratories, Paris (1928), and the Atomic Energy Research Centre, Saclay (1949). There have been many concrete churches, including Notre Dame at Le Raincy (1922) as one of the earliest, and St Joseph, Le Havre (1952); from his public buildings one might perhaps single out the Ecole Normale de Musique (1928) and the Musée des Travaux Publics (1938).

It is not easy to explain why certain countries—France, Switzerland, Germany and Italy particularly—should have adopted reinforced concrete so quickly, so enthusiastically and so successfully, and why others, notably Great Britain, should have hung behind. No doubt the peculiar nature of British architectural training, with its extreme conservatism and its tendency, until comparatively recently, to split off the engineer from the architect, has had something to do with it. So, too, have the British building regulations and the onetime obsession with something mysteriously known as 'finish'. While continental architects were finding patrons for their adventurous prestige buildings in concrete, steel, aluminium and glass, corresponding bodies in England were showing a marked inclination to regard these 'new' materials as unproved and with left-wing overtones. To some extent the critics and the disbelievers were right; much of the early concrete was extremely badly made and badly finished. Every country is littered with bits and pieces of crumbling, stained concrete dating from 1910–39. There is nothing attractive or commendable about a concrete canopy which has rotted away round the edges or a concrete bus shelter which has as a main feature the rust from the steel reinforcing rods. On the other hand it is perfectly fair to counter such examples by pointing to others which are well finished and have lasted well, even in the British climate, because both the architect and the builder knew what they were doing and made sure that their workmen were properly instructed and supervised.

The development of concrete as a building material during the past fifty years can be studied under three headings—new types of concrete, new structural and casting techniques and new kinds of concrete components—all of which are closely interrelated.

For more than half a century, attempts to reduce the cost of housing, especially working-class housing, have stimulated experiments to discover cheaper methods of building in concrete. During the 1920s, a good deal of interest was shown in what was called 'no-fines concrete' or 'cellular concrete', a special kind of poured concrete in which the ratio of cement to aggregate had been reduced to one in nine. Such concrete had a high proportion of voids and it needed plastering on both sides in order to produce an acceptable finish. But it was cheap and had good insulating properties. The earliest known examples of no-fines concrete buildings are a group of two-storey houses made with hard clinker aggregate at Scheveningen, Holland, in 1923. In Britain these were followed in 1923 by fifty two-storey houses in Edinburgh, also built with clinker aggregates. 'No-fines' concrete houses with clinker aggregate were built in a number of other places in Britain during the 1920s and 1930s, but the method has been little used for housing since 1939.[10]

Within the last twenty-five years concrete blocks have become one of the most used of all building materials. Some experience had already been gained before 1939 and during the war concrete blocks were used for a variety of simple, one-storey buildings needed by the military authorities. After the war, when materials were difficult to get and cost was once again an important factor, studies showed that walls built of reasonably light-weight concrete blocks could certainly be put up much faster than brick walls, and because cement was expensive and because block-making was on a much smaller scale than brick-making, the comparatively high cost of concrete blocks would usually more than offset the time saved in their erection.[11] Since that time, however, rising labour costs and manufacturing developments within the concrete industry itself have changed the situation in favour of the concrete block.

Simple, hand-operated, block-making machines were on the market by the end of the nineteenth century. In 1905 it was reckoned by a builder[12] that concrete blocks could be made on such a machine and

LIME, CEMENT, PLASTER AND CONCRETE

Figure 6 Concrete-block making machine *c.* 1860. The hand-operated mixer was moved from mould to mould. A gang of six men and a boy was required to operate the system, and produced 30–40 cubic yards of blocks a day or a much larger quantity of bulk concrete. A steam-driven machine was also available

laid more cheaply than brickwork, provided that his costs did not exceed the following limits:

Cement	38*s* a ton delivered
Aggregate	5*s* a ton delivered
Labourers	5*d* an hour
Blocklayer	9*d* an hour

This builder used the 'Pioneer' blockmaking machine, which cost him £80, and produced blocks 9 inches thick and 8, 16, 24 and 32 inches long. One of the largest blocks was equal to twenty-five bricks as it was really a small slab rather than a block in the sense in which the word is used nowadays.

British builders and architects have shown a strange reluctance to use hollow clay bricks and blocks, although such blocks have been available for many years and are much used on the Continent, especially for partition walls. The solid concrete block is viewed with much more favour.

The output of Portland cement in Britain trebled between 1945 and 1970 and the cost of production rose less than that of any other basic construction material, largely as a result of replacing the older, less efficient plants by modern automated units. To reduce costs, new plants have been sited away from the Thames–Medway area, in which most production was concentrated until the 1950s, and bulk transport by road or liner train to regional distribution depots or direct to large contracts has been used to rationalise supply and handling methods.

The huge and growing demand for aggregate has produced a difficult problem, especially in London and the south-east. The available supplies of gravel and crushed stone are nearing exhaustion in a number of areas, but alternative sources, such as gravel dredged from the sea-bed, have so far made it possible to meet requirements. Considerably ingenuity has been shown in discovering new aggregates. At Namur, in Belgium, for instance, the municipality now makes excellent concrete from household rubbish. The refuse first has its metal removed from it by means of an electromagnet, and is then ground and mixed with a small quantity of slag, calcium chloride, ferric sulphate, cement and water. It is then vibrated and pressed into hollow blocks, which are fully equal in strength to ordinary concrete blocks, but weigh less. They have good heat and noise insulating properties and can be sawn and nailed. Many other types of lightweight concrete are now on the market, using such waste materils as fly-ash.

The continuous development of placing equipment and form-work has reduced the demands on labour. The concrete mixer was invented as far back as 1857, by a French engineer, Louis Cézanne, and used by him in the construction of a bridge over the River Tisza in Hungary. The mixer worked on the modern principle, but was manually operated. The transit-mixer, mounted on a lorry, was first used in the United States in 1926 and is now an indispensible part of civil engineering equipment. Small-bore pumping units have recently come into widespread use for distributing concrete round the silo to ready-mix bricks. Mechanical vibration makes it possible to compact large masses of concrete in a way that was not previously possible.

Much attention has been given to reducing the cost of shuttering, by designing modular components which can be used repeatedly and moved rapidly to new sections of the work as soon as the concrete has begun to set. As concrete technology has advanced, the precast branch of the industry—organised since 1918 into the British Pre-Cast Concrete Federation—has greatly increased in importance. The precasting of concrete units, made away from the site under factory conditions, offers considerable technical and economic advantages: a high standard of quality control in manufacture; a degree of accuracy which is obtainable only with precision-built moulds and formwork; a more consistent product; and year-round production regardless of weather conditions.

Since 1960, there has been increasing use of factory-made concrete wall units. Such units are structural and often quite complicated. They may include an external facing, window frames, thermal insulation, an internal finish and conduits for plumbing and electric wiring. The prestressing of concrete is now a normal technique within the civil engineering field. The theory of prestressing was known at the end of the nineteenth century, but its application was not practicable at that time, because high tensile steel was not generally available. Fritz Dischinger used prestressing in bridge construction in Germany in 1928 and in the same year the French engineer, Eugène Freyssinet established the modern concept of the system. Prestressing is of particular value in the construction of load-bearing beams. By mechanical stretching of the high-tension reinforcing material, which is often piano wire, stresses are introduced into the concrete which are able to resist those of the external loading. The beams can consequently be made both stronger and lighter.

Fibreglass is being increasingly used, both for formwork and, more recently, as reinforcing material. Fibre-glass moulding allows concrete to be cast and finished with great accuracy and during the next twenty years alkali-resistant fibreglass reinforcement seems likely to bring about almost as great changes in the use of concrete as a building material as iron and steel did a century ago. Glass-reinforced cement and concrete seems certain to create many new building components and to replace some traditional ones. Its present applications are for sheet cladding and panels, thin, shaped sections, preformed permanent shuttering for cast concrete, cement-based spray coatings, pipes, posts and filing.

CHAPTER FIVE

Glass, Iron and Steel

Until the middle of the nineteenth century, most of the window glass used in England was crown-glass. It was made by taking a piece of molten glass, on the end of a blowing-iron and blowing it into a globe, reheating it and then spinning it out into a flat disc, which had what was known as a 'bull's-eye' in the middle. These discs, or 'tables' were from 40 inches to 5 feet in diameter. The larger sizes demanded great strength and skill on the part of the glass-blower. Crown glass had a very brilliant surface, but its quality varied a great deal and there were other disadvantages. As Henry Chance wrote in 1883, in his book, *The Principles of Glass-Making*: 'The cutting of a circle into rectangular sheets must, necessarily, be attended with waste, while the bull's-eye confines those sheets to comparatively small sizes. Uniformity of thickness, also, except by the most skilful manifestation, is difficult of attainment.'

Crown-glass was introduced into England from Normandy in the late seventeenth century. The name 'crown-glass' was given to it by John Bowles, or, at least, as a result of his method of embossing a crown in the centre of each pane produced at his glasshouse in London.

The cylinder method was developed in Lorraine and the Rhineland, probably during the fourteenth century. Here, too, the first step was to blow the glass into a sphere and then, by swinging the iron to and fro, to lengthen it into a cylinder. After reworking and reheating, the cylinder was cut along its length with shears and flattened in a furnace. The surface of the glass was smoothed by rubbing it with a wooden block which was fixed to the end of an iron rod. Glass made in this way was known in England as broad glass. It was reckoned to be inferior to crown-glass and mostly found its way into the houses of poorer people, especially in London, where it was brought by sea from the main centre of manufacture, Newcastle.

Plate glass, that is, glass made by casting, instead of blowing, was a

French development. The original invention was made by Bernard Perrot in 1687. Cast plate was first manufactured in England in 1773, at Ravenhead, St Helens, by the newly established British Cast Plate Glass Company, which was taken over in 1798 by the British Plate Glass Company. Part of the old casting hall still survives in what is now Pilkington's Ravenhead works.

Both the crown and the cylinder methods were greatly improved during the first half of the nineteenth century, but until 1845 progress was severely handicapped by the excise duty. This was first imposed in 1695, withdrawn in 1699, reimposed again in 1767 and finally repealed in 1845, after a Commission of Enquiry had revealed the effects the duty was having on the industry. The system was complicated as well as punitive. Three types of duty were payable: an annual licence for each glasshouse; a payment for each pound of glass melted in the pots and ready for use; and, most remarkable of all, a payment per pound on the excess in weight of manufactured glass over 40 per cent of the calculated weight of molten glass. Two excise officers were allocated to each glassworks to make sure the regulations were observed, and as one manufacturer put it, in his evidence to the Commissioners of Excise: 'Our business premises are placed under the arbitrary control of a class of men to whose will and caprice it is most irksome to have to submit, and it is under a system of regulations most ungraciously inquisitorial. We cannot enter parts of our own premises without their permission.'[1]

There is no doubt that it was the high rate of excise duty which caused Britain to be so slow in adopting sheet glass, in place of crown. The duty was levied by weight, but the glass was sold by size and quality. The manufacturer therefore had every incentive to make his panes as thin as possible and crown glass, which was spun, could be made thinner than sheet, which was blown. Before 1845 a high proportion of British sheet glass was exported. It was profitable to do this, since for every hundredweight of glass on which £3 13s 6d was paid in duty, the manufacturer recovered £4 18s 0d from the Excise authorities for glass exported in the form of panes. The figures for British sheet glass exported and retained for home consumption in 1834 and 1844 illustrate the situation.[2]

The introduction of cylinder glass to the British market in the 1830s and 1840s was of great importance to the glass industry. In 1845, when the duty was finally abolished, firms such as Pilkington's,

BUILDING MATERIALS

Year	Exports cwt.	Home consumption cwt.	Total production of crown glass cwts.
1834	5343	nil	131,365
1844	7703	23,857	104,340

which had already established cylinder glass departments had a great advantage over those who had restricted themselves to the production of crown glass.

After the glass duty was abolished, the cost of glass fell rapidly. By 1849 the price was about a quarter of what it had been five years earlier. This was caused mainly by the disappearance of the duty, but also by the removal of the import duties on foreign glass. Even after 1845, however, the building industry continued to be hampered for some years by the window tax.

The window tax was levied only on houses, not on industrial or commercial premises. The tax was paid by the occupier, not the owner, and was on a sliding scale. The rates increased steadily between 1766 and 1808.

	1766 tax	1808 tax
Houses with 7 windows	1s 2d	20s
Houses with 8 windows	4s	33s
Houses with 9 windows	6s	42s

and continuing on a rising scale, according to the number of windows. The rates were halved in 1823 and in 1825 the seventh window was exempted. The tax was abolished in 1851.

The repeal of the excise duty gave architects a great incentive to design buildings which used glass on a completely different scale. The pioneer in this field was Sir Joseph Paxton, who was gardener to the Duke of Devonshire and revolutionised the construction of conservatories and greenhouses at Chatsworth. Paxton's first great work, the Chatsworth Conservatory (1838–40) was built while glass was still extremely expensive. It was a glass palace, 277 feet long, 132 feet broad, and 67 feet high. The framework and glazing bars were very slender and the glass used was sheet, in unprecedented lengths of 4 feet, made by an improved cylinder process introduced by Robert Lucas Chance from the Continent. When Paxton made his first approach to Chance he was told that 3 feet was the maximum length which could be made.

I was advised (he recalled afterwards) to use this glass in two lengths with one overlap, but to this I could not assent; as I observed that since they had so far advanced as to be able to produce sheets three feet in length, I saw no reason why they should not accomplish another foot; and if this could not be done, I would decline giving the order, as, at that time, sheet glass was altogether an experiment in horticultural purposes. These gentlemen, however, shortly afterwards informed me that they had one person who could make it the desired length, and if I would give the order they would furnish all I desired.[3]

Chance's experiment with this contract allowed them to supply within a very short period—63,000 panes, each 49 by 10 inches were made in a single fortnight—a total of nearly a million square feet of glass for the Crystal Palace, built in 1850-51 for the Great Exhibition, and a further three-quarters of a million when the building was re-erected at Sydenham in 1852. Paxton's design depended on an iron framework and a new type of wooden sashbar, which allowed both glazing and repair work to be carried out very rapidly. One glazier fitted 108 panes in a day.

In his book, *What is to become of the Crystal Palace?*, Paxton emphasised that the abolition of the glass duty had brought about a complete change, both for architects and for gardeners.

The removal of the duty on glass [he wrote] has given an impetus to this science [horticulture] which only a short time ago no efforts could possibly have called into action; indeed, had that duty still existed, no building such as I am now treating of could possibly have been erected, and without an extensive use of glass to equally admit and diffuse a subdued light, no such display as at present could have been secured.

Since that time new developments in the glass industry have provided the architect and the builder with the basis of a series of important technical innovations. The first commercially successful manufacture of wired-glass was begun by Pilkingtons in 1898. Glass blocks or bricks made their appearance in Germany at about the same time and in 1900 the Germans started manufacturing 'glass-silk', a material commercially developed by Pilkingtons in the 1930s. Toughened glass, for use in doors and partitions, was introduced in

1928. Another major Pilkington invention, the float glass process, in which glass is continuously cast on a bed of molten tin, dates from 1952.

Progress in the use of glass, metal frames and concrete has been closely interlinked. Morton Shand has pointed out that:

> The need for standardised sections was felt, however dimly, long before machinery for producing them existed. The rail preceded the girder as the street precedes the house. The triumph of the railways inculcated a growing consciousness of the universal adaptability of iron. Cast-iron was the precursor of steel in most of the uses for which the latter is now almost exclusively employed.[4]

By 1800 cast iron columns were being widely used in the design of factories, churches and theatres and in the first quarter of the nineteenth century verandahs and balconies included a good deal of structural iron. French architects and engineers were prominent in these developments. A metal-framed market, the Marché de la Madeleine, was built in Paris in 1824, and Fontaine's Galerie d'Orléans (1829), also in Paris, was one of the first buildings to have a glass and iron roof. This elegant shopping arcade, pulled down in 1935, was imitated a good deal in Italy, especially in Milan.

One of the earliest English examples of iron and glass construction was the Fish Market (1835), built on the site of the present Charing Cross railway station. This light, graceful building consisted of nothing more than a roof, supported by hollow iron columns, which also functioned as drains for the roof-water. At the same time, iron construction was being adopted for conservatories. Among these iron-framed conservatories of the 1830s were those at Syon House, Alton Towers, the seat of the Earl of Shrewsbury, eight miles from Uttoxeter, and The Grange, three miles from Alresford, in Hampshire, the last of this group being built for Lord Ashburton by Sir Charles Cockerell.

Experiment continued during the 1840s. Paxton's conservatory at Chatsworth has already been mentioned. Other impressive iron-framed glass-houses of this decade were the Palm House at Kew (1844–46) and the Conservatory of the Royal Botanical Society (1846), both by Decimus Burton and Richard Turner, and the Riding School at Welbeck (1850). Turner was the proprietor of the Hammersmith Iron Works, Dublin, and described himself as 'Designer and Contractor for wrought iron conservatories, roofs of railway termini and other purposes, and hot water engineer'. One of his contracts was for the roof of Lime Street Station, Liverpool (1854), which had a curved roof, with single spans of over 153 feet. The glazing was carried out in sheets measuring 12 feet 4 inches by 3 feet 6 inches, but there was no allowance for expansion and contraction and there was continuous trouble with broken panes until the roof was renewed in 1959.

Another notable station roof was at New Street, Birmingham (1854). This was 840 feet long and had a clear span of 212 feet. There was glazing along the centre and at both sides, with the remainder covered with corrugated iron. The gable ends of the roof were closed by glass screens, each weighing 30 tons. King's Cross (1852) originally had a timber-framed roof, with iron glazing-bars. This was replaced by an iron and glass roof in two stages, 1869 and 1886.

Among the other notable public buildings of the nineteenth century which included glass and iron roofs were the Royal Exchange and the Coal Exchange, both in London. The roof at the Royal Exchange (1880) was designed by Sir Charles Barry and has a central dome. The Coal Exchange (1846–49) in Lower Thames Street was the work of James Bunning, the City Architect. It was demolished in the 1950s, despite a long campaign to save it. Henry-Russell Hitchcock, in his book, *Early Victorian Architecture in Britain*, has described it as 'the prime City monument of the Early Victorian Period'. 'The use of an interior iron skeleton,' he goes on, 'received nowhere so completely integrated an architectural expression as in its glass-domed court.'

During the nineteenth century there were many attempts to improve on the usual method of bedding the glass in putty on iron or wooden glazing bars, with the aim of cutting down maintenance costs. These innovations included galvanised wrought iron sash bars —the Adam brothers had used bronze for this purpose in the eighteenth century—and various types of patent glazing which eliminated the need for putty.

Once architects had learnt to design buildings in which the weight was carried on a steel or concrete frame, instead of on the external walls, it became possible to use much lighter materials for cladding. Glass was an obvious choice for this. The Tietz department store in Berlin (1896) had a plateglass façade running up all four storeys and other early applications of this technique were the Hallidie Building in San Francisco (1918), the Nelle factory (1924) and the De Bijenkorf store (1930) in Rotterdam and the machine shops at the Bauhaus, Dessau (1926). Le Corbusier's Salvation Army hostel in Paris, the Cité de Refuge (1933), has a glass curtain wall covering almost the whole of the south front of the main building. Air-conditioning obviates the need to have any opening windows. The first English building seriously to approach the curtain wall method of construction was the Peter Jones store (1936) in London. The façade consists of vertical ranges of metal windows, fixed between steel mullions. The casements between the floors open, to allow the glass to be easily cleaned. External treatments of this kind were possible only after the introduction of metal windows, which became commercially practicable after the invention of the metal extrusion process (1893) and the development of hot rolling processes for the production of light metal sections. Standard-sized windows in steel, aluminium, bronze and stainless alloys have given architects a completely new type of component to work with.

Boots's factory (1930-2) at Nottingham has steel framed glazed walls and a glass and concrete roof. The *Daily Express* building (1932) in London is faced with black toughened glass and the Troy Court block of flats in Kensington uses opal glass to cover brickwork.

Curtain walls are usually glazed by bedding the glass in putty or a mastic, which has to be maintained to keep the building weather-resistant. Many specialised types of mastic are now on the market. They include thiokol and neoprene, which are based on synthetic rubber. These materials can be injection-moulded to produce a continuous one-piece gasket, with an estimated life of twenty-five years. The gaskets provide a cushion against expansion and vibration, as well as a seal against the weather.

The inclusion of glass lenses in reinforced concrete domes and vaults has been an important twentieth-century development. It is an extension of the cellar light and of the 'illuminations' which were being fitted in the decks of ships during the early years of last century. The first cellar lights consisted of a thick slab of cast glass, fixed either directly in stone or bedded into an iron frame. The metal-framed pavement light, with cut squares or lenses of glass fitted into a grid, dates from the 1880s. In recent years the practice has been to

25 The old method of converting logs. Pit-sawyers at Terling, Essex

26 Seasoning timber in the traditional way, Terling, Essex

27 Roof timbering in the machine shop, Railway Works, Swindon

28 Laminated roof construction in a worsted mill, Bradford

use smaller lenses fitted into reinforced concrete. These withstand heavy traffic loads without damage.

The first glass and concrete roof-lights in Britain were put into the Kodak factory (1910) at Wealdstone and into Whiteley's store (1910) in London. Since then there have been a number of technical improvements, mostly aimed at preventing the cracking of unprotected concrete surfaces and at sealing the joint between the glass and the concrete, where shrinkage and leakage are most likely to occur. The concrete, glass and asphalt roof gives satisfactory results.

Glass bricks became available about 1900. They are very useful for partition walls in areas where very careful attention has to be paid to lighting. Modern glass bricks include an air-space to increase insulation. Prismatic bricks are also available, to reduce glare.

Toughening glass has greatly widened the range of applications to which glass can be put. The toughening process is a form of pre-stressing which counteracts the tensile weakness of the surface of ordinary glass. The process consists essentially of heating the glass almost to the point of plasticity and then cooling it rapidly by means of jets of cold air. The resulting glass is very resistant to shock and to heat. It is widely used in industry, on ships and for frameless doors.

In discussing the history of glass as a building material we are bound to be thinking at the same time of the structures which held the glass in position and this, for the nineteenth century means that we are considering glass and iron together, both being units of repetitive dimensions and the two in combination contributing to a new type of architecture, characterised by a high degree of prefabrication.

It has been pointed out[5] that in 1840 when people talked of iron in bridges and buildings they invariably meant cast iron. Yet only ten years later engineers almost invariably made major beams or girders of wrought iron. For these purposes, cast iron had been completely superseded. Cast iron, however, continued to retain its usefulness for purposes which belonged to the builder rather than the civil engineer, although it is, of course, impossible to fix a firm dividing line between the two.

A furniture store in Macclesfield, built in the 1870s, has its façade entirely in cast iron and glass, and has a light, graceful appearance which contrasts sharply with that of a four-storey mill by the side of the Rochdale Canal at Todmorden. The mill, built between 1880 and

1890 is a much heavier looking building. The construction has cast iron columns, carrying wooden beams and floors and it is faced with a grid of prefabricated cast iron strips, which enclose wooden windows.

Prefabricated iron components have been used by English builders since the early eighteenth century, the first examples being railings and balconies. Cast iron railings were fixed around St Paul's Cathedral in 1714. They were cast at Lamberhurst and consisted of 2650 pieces.[6] Similar railings were made for St Martin-in-the-Fields in the 1720s. By the 1770s many different designs of cast iron gates and railings could be obtained commercially. The architect, Robert Adam, who had connexions with the Carron Ironworks at Falkirk, produced a design which was well-suited to balcony railings cast in quantity. In 1815 John Nash designed cast iron staircases which can still be seen for the extension of Brighton Pavilion. The balustrades were made to imitate bamboo. In the 1820s iron-works began to manufacture cast iron helical staircases, which were very popular in Victorian shops, warehouses and offices.

Supplying builders' ironmongery and brassware became an important business for many manufacturers during the nineteenth century. Most of these components were small—locks, bolts, hinges and window-fastenings—but, together with grates and cooking ranges, in total they represented a considerable annual value. Iron window frames were already being made in the last few years of the eighteenth century and early in the nineteenth. They can be seen in many of the textile mills which survive from this period, being very common in Gloucestershire and Wiltshire.

By 1900 builders were using what was termed 'combination ranges', coal-burning ranges both for cooking and for providing a supply of hot water. They were made of cast iron and were permanently built into a brick surround. An unusually elaborate example of such a range was Corne's Combination Range, introduced about 1900, which had a bath in the same room. Other ranges incorporated a copper for washing clothes.

Iron was the only material, apart from glass, which was extensively used for prefabrication before 1900. Victorian builders trusted it and understood it. The designers of many office buildings, banks and department stores made use of prefabricated cast iron panels and windows. These iron components have often been obscured by subsequent painting and surface treatment, as at 415–419 Oxford Street,

London. This building, between Duke Street and Lumley Street, was completed in 1925. It has a cast iron front, backed with $4\frac{1}{2}$ inches of concrete. In other buildings, such as the Liverpool Cotton Exchange (1853), the iron panels and windows were left more obvious and unashamed.

CHAPTER SIX

Timber, Plywood and Wood Products

During the past fifty years timber has passed from being one of the cheapest and most easily obtainable of all building materials to one which is expensive and in short supply. This is the inevitable result of an almost criminally wasteful misuse of resources in the main timber-producing countries, where forests have been ruthlessly cleared, with little attempt to replant, and of a lack of foresight in the importing countries, such as Britain, where a determined afforestation policy during the period between the wars would have made it possible to meet something like 95 per cent of our present requirements of softwoods from home production. As it is, timber has been increasingly pricing itself out of the market for twenty-five years and, for constructional uses, it must now in many countries be considered almost a luxury material.

Against this background, the consumption of timber for building purposes during previous centuries appears almost unbelievably prodigal. It is useful to work out an approximate cost, at today's prices, of the oak used in the construction of the half-timbered houses common in England in the fifteenth, sixteenth and seventeenth centuries. If it could be obtained in the sizes, shapes and quality needed, the oak for the framing and roof-timber of a modest sized farmhouse would nowadays cost at least £20,000. What was once the commonest of building materials has now become an expensive imported luxury and modern architects do everything possible to avoid using it.

In some countries this has always been so. Timber has always been a relatively scarce commodity in Denmark and the Netherlands, for example. In others—Canada, Norway and Sweden are good examples —it is still sufficiently plentiful to allow it to continue to be a first choice for most domestic building.

For the whole of the eighteenth and nineteenth centuries timber seemed inexhaustible in the United States, and it was felled, used and exported in what now seems the most wasteful and reckless fashion. It remained the dominant material for industrial and railway structures until the middle of the nineteenth century and it is still very widely used for ordinary family housing. The cheapness of timber and the high cost of iron caused American engineers to use wood at a time when Europeans chose iron as a normal practice. Large and elaborate timber bridges, for instance, were being constructed in the United States as late as the 1850s, with ingenious trusses to enable very heavy loads to be taken across rivers and ravines. The techniques evolved for these timber trusses were later transferred to steel, so that many of the American railway bridges of the second half of the century had a timber look about them.

The early settlers in America took the tradition of the medieval framed house with them, but during the eighteenth century it became increasingly difficult to find the massive timbers required for the old type of construction and, as the population increased and demand grew, some way had to be found of achieving the same degree of strength in house-building with machine-cut timber of much smaller sections. This was achieved by the development of what is known as the balloon-frame, in which heavy timbers were replaced by a large number of light boards nailed together to make a rigid cage of sills, floors, joists, upright posts and roof rafters. In addition to the rectangular system of vertical and horizontal members, there were usually diagonal pieces fastened across the lower corners of the wall frame to provide strengthening against wind loads. The outside of the frame was covered with weatherboarding.

This type of housing, like the timber engineering to which reference has already been made, would not have been possible without cheap, mass-produced nails. It is not surprising, therefore, that the Americans were to the forefront in the development of nail-making machinery. The first American patent seems to be that of Ezekiel Reed, in 1786. Before the end of the century machines fed with mild steel wire were capable of turning out 300 nails a minute, the cutting and pointing being carried out simultaneously. Wood screws were being made by machine and on a factory basis in the 1760s, by the brothers Job and William Wyatt at two workshops in Staffordshire.[1] For many years, however, it was only possible to make screws with a blunt point. Pointed screws were first made in America during the 1830s and in the 1840s. America also pioneered automatic machines for making screws. These were exhibited at the Great Exhibition in London in 1851 and installed by Nettlefold and Chamberlain at their factory in Birmingham in 1854.

By no means all the nineteenth-century innovations in timber construction and engineering took place in America. The Swiss and the Austrians were famous for their large timber bridges as early as the 1780s, and some of the finest timber engineering to be seen in any country was carried out by Brunel in the construction of his railway bridge.[2] He used timber for a number of early bridges, on the Bristol and South Wales lines and worked out experiments to determine the strength of wooden beams and to find out the best techniques for preserving them. His main achievements with timber bridges were on the South Devon and Cornish lines, where there were many deep valleys to be crossed and where the traffic did not justify the expense of masonry or wrought iron structures. There were thirty-four of these viaducts between Plymouth and Truro alone. Brunel had originally intended to take the railway over the Tamar at Saltash by means of a timber bridge, but the Admiralty's regulations made this impossible. Had the project succeeded, it would have been the largest timber bridge in the world, with six spans of 100 feet and one of 250 feet.

For his later bridges on the Tavistock branch and in West Cornwall Brunel worked to a standardised design, with two spans, one of 66 feet and the other of 50 feet. This allowed him to use standard units of timber and to carry out maintenance much more quickly. Over tidal creeks, the bridges were carried on timber trestles, but inland they rested on stone piers, each with four tapering buttresses. They were beautiful structures; L. T. C. Rolt's description catches both the genius and the simplicity of them:

> On the tops of these buttresses (he notes) rested cast iron caps from which the timber beams sprang like the four outspread fingers of a hand to support the main longitudinal timbers. These main timbers, which carried the platform, consisted of two baulks set one above the other and joggled together so that their combined strength was almost equal to that of a continuous beam. Cross and diagonal timber ties and iron tie rods completed the structure. At the approaches there were no massive wing walls or abutments. King trusses at each end rested upon simple masonry

platforms so that the bridges would not be affected by any settlement of the approach embankments. A simpler or more graceful design or one better calculated to become a part of the *genius loci* of the region it would be hard to conceive. In the primeval, storm-bitter landscape of western Cornwall the tapering piers of local stone looked as much at home as the gaunt chimney stacks of the tin mines. So nicely was the proportion of each beam and truss adjusted to the load which it would bear that the effect was one of a lightness and fragility so remarkable that it looked incapable of supporting even the lightest of locomotives. Indeed it was for this reason that, when the Cornwall Railway was opened, the local people displayed a marked reluctance to travel over it and time alone conquered their fear of the viaducts.[3]

All Brunel's viaducts in Devon and Cornwall were built of the best quality yellow pine from Memel in the Baltic. These timbers lasted up to sixty years. When the railway was built, Baltic pine was plentiful and cheap, but by 1900 it had become unobtainable and when the main line to Penzance was doubled in 1908 the original timber viaducts were replaced by the present steel and masonry structures. Many of the old piers remain, however, by the side of the line in use today, and the Royal Cornwall Institution in Truro has a complete set of photographs, showing the Cornish viaducts as Brunel built them.

It is curious to notice that Britain was very backward in the introduction of saw-milling machinery. This must have been due partly to the abundance of labour which was available to carry out the task by hand and partly to the fact that, by contrast with such countries as Sweden and Germany, England used relatively little timber for building. Germany certainly had water-driven sawmills in the fourteenth century and Norway and Sweden in the sixteenth. In the American colonies, labour was always in short supply and water-power was used to drive saws from at least the middle of the seventeenth century and probably earlier. There was violent opposition to the establishment of a sawmill in London in 1663.

In 1767 or 1768, when an opulent timber-merchant, by the desire and approbation of the Society of Arts, caused a saw-mill, driven by the wind, to be erected at Limehouse under the direction of James Stansfield, who had learned, in Holland and Norway, the art of constructing and managing machines of that kind. A mob assembled, and pulled the mill to pieces; but the damage was made good by the nation, and some of the rioters were punished. A new mill was afterwards erected, which was suffered to work without molestation, and which gave occasion to the erection of others.[4]

The development of plywood has been closely linked to the availability of suitable machinery and adhesives. A sheet of plywood is no more nor less than a number of thin veneers, glued together with the grain of the adjacent veneers running in different directions. The craft of veneering was rediscovered early in the seventeenth century. The great eighteenth-century cabinet-makers of France and England used veneers with wonderful skill to create magnificent furniture, but during the nineteenth century veneering acquired a bad name, as a result of the extensive use of veneers on cheap furniture in order to hide defective construction.

Until the second half of the nineteenth century veneers were nearly always cut with saws, a task demanding great skill and accuracy, although in some cases they were obtained by slicing, the timber being passed under a fixed knife held in the machine. Plywoods were certainly in use by the 1840s, and probably earlier, but for many years the master cabinet-makers alone appear to have made use of the principle that wood could be given extra strength by glueing three pieces together, the middle pieces laid with the grain across. In 1844 a small factory at Revel in Esthonia applied this theory to the construction of seats for bentwood chairs, using birch or beech for the purpose. Soon after the Civil War several Americans took out patents for laminating layers of wood veneer, putting the grain of one layer at right-angles to the next. Early in the 1870s George Gardner of Brooklyn began making plywood benches for railway stations and other public places. The curves were obtained by bending the material under steam. When knife-cutting machines became available, about 1890, an altogether different technique was employed. Instead of the log being sawn across, it was rotated against a knife-edge, so that a continuous veneer was produced, very much like unrolling a Swiss-roll. This gave large sheets of veneer, in place of the narrow strips from the old process, and it soon became apparent that by using these large veneers plywood boards of previously impossible size and strength could be built up.

The first big customers for plywood were the tea-shippers, who were using the now familiar tea-chests by the mid 1890s. The commercial three-ply board followed soon afterwards. By 1914 there were a number of factories producing plywood on a large scale in various parts of Europe, especially in the Scandinavian and Baltic countries, some to meet the growing demand for three-ply tea-chests and packing-cases, and others to manufacture specially faced boards for the cabinet-makers.

Very rapid advances in the technique of plywood manufacture were made during the 1914–18 war, when the aircraft industry required large quantities of thin plywood of a higher quality than had been previously available. The main problem was the adhesive. The waterproof glues evolved by chemists in Europe and America during the First World War improved the strength and reliability of plywood to such an extent that by the 1920s it had lost its old reputation of being a cheap, but inferior substitute for solid wood, and became accepted as a useful and even fashionable material in its own right.

Plywood should be distinguished from laminated timber. The essential difference between the two is that in the case of laminated timber the grain of all the layers runs in the same direction, whereas in plywood alternate layers are cross-grained. There is the further difference that laminated timber, as the term is usually understood, is usually designed for beams, arches and other substantial structural units.

Several layers of timber were often bolted together, and sometimes glued as well for added strength, in nineteenth-century building work, but the British laminated timber industry really dates from the years immediately after the end of the war in 1945, when there was a serious shortage of structural steel and an urgent need both to repair damage caused by bombing and to catch up with arrears in building. One of the most spectacular examples of laminated construction during this period was the group of parabolic arches made from Douglas fir which were erected at Waterloo Station as part of the Festival of Britain celebrations.[5] The techniques which were needed for this type of work had been accumulated to some extent by the wartime requirement for naval mine-sweepers built entirely of wood to counteract the threat of magnetic mines. This led to the creation of special production units throughout the country. A similar body of experience had been built up in the factories which made aircraft propellers from laminated blocks.

In Britain, progress with laminated constructional timbers was greatly handicapped for many years by the *British Standard Code of Practice* C.P. 112 (1952), *The Structural Use of Timber in Buildings*. This deals almost entirely with the properties of sawn timber, but the recommendations of the Code were incorporated in the building bye-laws, with the result that the design of structures in laminated timber had to follow those for sawn timber. This meant that the advantages of laminated timber could not be fully exploited and that, in consequence, timber was wastefully used. Broadly speaking, where there are no knots laminated timber has no advantage over sawn timber. When knots are present the situation is different, because the knots are limited in depth by the thickness of the laminations and do not extend right through the structural member.[6]

The use of wood as a building material has been revolutionised by the developments of new types of adhesive. Until the second half of the nineteenth century all that was available to stick two pieces of wood together was the substance known to joiners and cabinet makers as glue, made by rendering down animal bones, horns and hoofs. This had to be reheated each time it was required and had the great disadvantage of becoming weakened by contact with water and by the growth of fungus and micro-organisms, so that timber could only be used for structural purposes when it was jointed mechanically, by means of bolts, screws or nails, and by the growth of fungus and micro-organisms. During the past forty years synthetic resins have changed the situation completely. Urea formaldehyde resins are the cheapest of all the synthetic resins. They are widely used in the manufacture of plywood and various kinds of building board, and also for making flush doors and furniture.

These resins have found a major market since 1945 in the manufacture of what is technically known as particle board, made by chipping or shredding wood, mixing it with resin and pressing it into large boards. This industry has developed from the original concept of a means of using waste wood to a major manufacturing industry for which wood is specially grown. Urea formaldehyde resins represent about 6 per cent of the weight of the board.

These urea formaldehyde glues represent a major step forward in the technology of timber glueing, but their resistance to moisture is not adequate for making plywood which is to be used externally. For this purpose it is necessary to use phenolic resin glues, which produce a grade of plywood which is water and boil proof and is called WBP plywood for this reason. These superior plywoods are often referred to as exterior grades. They have been much used for concrete framework for a number of years and they now form an important component in composite panels for factory-built timber houses.

Phenolic resins for making plywood are of the hot-setting type and are not suitable for workshop use. The resorcinol formaldehyde resins, which are related chemically to the phenolic resins, are much easier to handle, provided the workshop is kept at a minimum temperature of 21°C. Very large timber structures can be made with these adhesives but they are just as valuable for the construction of simple prefabricated roof trusses, decks and box beams.

An earlier form of building board, introduced under the names of pulpboard or millboard, originated in Britain. It was the invention of D. M. Sutherland, who had been experimenting in Edinburgh with processes for manufacturing boards from wood waste. Sutherland founded the Patent Millboard Company at Sunbury-on-Thames in 1898. He built up a good export trade to the United States, where millboard was manufactured from 1909 onwards and later improved to make a harder, tougher material, fibre-board.[7] These boards contain no resin as a bonding agent and are suitable only in situations where they can be protected from damp.

The present use of timber for building purposes is conditioned by its high cost. The more of the tree that can be used, the lower the cost will be and the growth of the building board industry as a way of making profitable use of waste and low-grade wood has consequently been of great importance. Until very recently builders thought only in terms of natural timber, sawn to the dimensions required, and the individual qualities of each consignment were vital. The best timber had been well grown, felled at the right time of year, allowed to dry naturally in the log and then seasoned after sawing until it was in ideal condition for use. This ideal became impossible to maintain as world demand grew. The trees were felled, processed and sold with the maximum speed possible, artificial drying being used as a matter of course. Kiln drying of timber, introduced in the 1870s, is now accepted practice for all but the most expensive hardwoods, and modern methods allow the process to be controlled with great exactness, at least for boards and similarly thin sections.

With large timbers, kiln drying is less successful and some very unpleasant splitting and twisting can be seen in much of the timber used as beams and posts in post-1945 building projects. The contrast with the wonderful timber-engineering in such substantial buildings as the Assembly Hall at Cheltenham Ladies College and the main railway station in Copenhagen is most marked. Built with seasoned pine, these old structures are still in excellent condition.

The different parts of the British Isles have not been equally kind to old timber. Broadly speaking, decay as a result of beetle, worm and fungus is much worse on the western side of the country. Rentokil, Britain's leading specialists in the preservation of building timbers, estimate that, if it has not been scientifically treated, about 80 per cent of the structural woodwork in the western counties is affected by some form of infestation or disease, compared with about 30 per cent in the eastern counties, a fact borne out by building society surveys. Under some conditions, however, the normal pattern of decay does not operate so ferociously. Two of the finest nineteenth-century timber roofs in the West Country, in I. K. Brunel's original station at Temple Meads, Bristol, and in the old machine shop at the Railway Works, Swindon, are still in excellent condition, probably because there is no ceiling and the ventilation around the timbers is therefore exceptionally good. The same is true of the massive timber frames in No. 53 (1813) and No. 60 (1837) Boat Stores at Chatham Dockyard, and Slip No. 1 (1772) at Devonport.

Curiously, one of the most durable ways of using timber has been as weatherboard cladding. When kept regularly painted, with the roof and guttering in good condition, timber weatherboard has a remarkably long life, even in the British climate. Weatherboarded buildings are especially common in the east and south-east, where there are many beautiful surviving examples, Bocking Mill and Coggleshall Mills in Essex, and Horstead Mill at Coltishall, Norfolk, for example, together with many houses in the villages of West Kent and East Sussex. Nowhere has timber given better value or more pleasure to the eye.

CHAPTER SEVEN

Some Major New Materials

Aluminium
It is only since 1945 that aluminium[1] has come to be generally accepted as a building material, though the first applications of the metal in this field were made as long ago as the 1890s, only a few years after commercial production became possible. The cupola of the Church of San Gioacchino in Rome was covered with aluminium sheet in 1897. This roofing—the earliest known use of aluminium for the purpose—was still in good condition when it was examined in 1949. Sir Alfred Gilbert's cast-aluminium statue of Eros, at Piccadilly Circus, was set up there is 1893 and has withstood the London atmosphere wonderfully well, with no appreciable deterioration.

San Gioacchino was an architectural freak. Up to 1914 aluminium was used mainly for pots and pans. The building industry began to think seriously about it in the early 1930s, when the extrusion process made it possible to produce aluminium glazing bars at a reasonable price. This was one of the first applications where the combination of strength and high corrosion resistance possessed by aluminium was used to maximum advantage. Aluminium lends itself very well to extrusion, and the production of glazing bars by this method allowed more complex and more efficient shapes to be designed. Condensation channels and special glazing devices are incorporated in the one extrusion.

Apart from this very successful development, most of the aluminium that went into building before 1939 consisted of decorative metal-work, mostly internal. For expensive prestige buildings, however, architects allowed themselves more freedom to experiment. The Friends Provident and Century Life Office (1933) in Corn Street, Bristol, has aluminium window and door frames, anodised to a natural finish, which are still in excellent condition. Sir Giles Gilbert Scott specified aluminium window frames for the extensions to the

Bodleian Library, Oxford (1939) and the Cambridge University Library (1939).

At the end of the war, in 1945, both the aluminium and the aircraft industries found themselves with a greatly increased production capacity and the need to find new outlets. Housing was one obvious answer, and 78,000 aluminium bungalows were built between 1945 and 1948, mostly for the Ministry of Works. Many of these houses are still in service, although they were originally designed for a life of only ten years. For the most part, they made use of aircraft scrap, which was readily available at the time. This re-used alloy does not have the same life as the virgin metal, but it has shown itself capable of much longer service than was originally expected.

For these prefabricated bungalows, aluminium was used in two forms, extrusion and clad-sheet—strong aluminium alloy which is given a superior resistance to corrosion by coating it with a layer of the pure metal. Shallow box wall frames were filled with foamed concrete and faced internally with plaster-board. The roof was made of toughened clad sheet, supported on alloy trusses, under which was carried a fibre-board ceiling. The window frames, too, were of alloys but timber was used for the doors, door-frames and floors. The structural subsections—floor, walls, spinal partition and roof—were assembled and despatched complete with all the fittings, wiring and plumbing. Each bungalow contained about $1\frac{3}{4}$ tons of aluminium sheet, strip, extrusions and castings.

The bungalows, which were made by a number of firms, were useful experimental projects and provided experience for a number of successful later developments. They allowed one principle to be clearly established. Since, volume for volume, the cost of aluminium is about two and a half times that of steel, the designer has to aim at the minimum use of material. To achieve this, he uses extruded sections which exactly meet the conditions of service. These can be very thin, in the knowledge that they will not deteriorate under atmospheric attack. In order to economise in his expensive material, he is justified in taking great pains over design and in using relatively expensive production techniques.

The original bungalows were followed by many other types, some entirely of aluminium, some with the structure only of aluminium. Most of them were for export, especially to tropical or subtropical countries, and were designed for easy transport in difficult country and for erection by unskilled labour. For one project, 186 fully insulated single-storey buildings were produced to house the communities working on oil surveys in Argentina. No unit weighed more than 140 pounds. They were assembled to form living-bungalows, offices, canteens and stores and after each two-year survey they were dismantled, transported to fresh territory and re-erected.

During the 1940s a great deal was learnt about the use of aluminium in structural engineering. It was realised that the advantages of aluminium could best be exploited on very large spans, in which the dead weight becomes a much greater proportion of the load. To begin with, aluminium was used for the trusses, with the stanchions of concrete or steel, but it was later found possible to carry out the whole job in aluminium, using, as the uprights, extruded hollow box-shaped sections, 6 inches by 3 inches.

An important milestone was the hangar—the first aluminium hangar in Britain—designed in 1951 for London Airport. The acceptance of aluminium by the Ministry of Civil Aviation was a great step forward after many years of trying to convince engineers, planning authorities and the Government of its reliability as a structural medium.

Aluminium has been used a great deal in the construction of aeroplane hangars. One of the most striking is the Brabazon Assembly Hall at Filton, Bristol. The structure is of steel, but aluminium was used for the roof-glazing and for the enormous doors, which would hardly have been feasible in any other material. They are 65 feet 9 inches high and a total of 1045 feet long. The 32 folding leaves are made almost entirely of aluminium sheet and extrusions. They weigh 200 tons and can be opened in two minutes.

An obvious application of aluminium to structural engineering is where a new structure has to be erected on top of an existing building. An interesting example of this was the addition of a fourth storey to the Radcliffe Infirmary, Oxford, in 1952. If the framework for this had been fabricated in steel, it would have weighed 20 tons and would have seriously overloaded the existing brick building. The aluminium structure weighed only 12 tons, which was within the limit which the existing building could support.

One of the early difficulties in the use of aluminium as a structural material was that there was no agreed Code of Practice, and therefore no standards on which to base specifications for a building or structure in aluminium and no basis for approving designs. Aluminium, as a structural material, was not referred to in the building bye-laws. In 1950, as a first step towards rectifying this very unsatisfactory situation, the Institution of Structural Engineers produced its *Report on the Structural Use of Aluminium Alloys in Buildings*. The new model bye-laws which were subsequently adopted by local authorities included aluminium as an accepted structural material, providing the design and fabrication was in accordance with the Report.

Another important development of the 1940s was the manufacture of prefabricated schools. Modular components were used and the units were suitable for a wide range of school buildings. The wall panels were 4 feet wide and in 4 heights, according to the type of room. They were clad externally with ribbed aluminium sheet, and internally with wallboard and filled with fibre-glass insulation. A wall panel could either have no windows or be entirely glazed.

During the 1950s and 1960s the range of applications of aluminium in building has been greatly widened. It has become a popular material for roofing and wall facing, although, for some unexplained reason, it is still less used for the purpose in Britain than in America or on the Continent. Aluminium window-frames, corrugated sheeting and roof-trusses are being increasingly used, especially in highly corrosive atmospheres, where long life and low maintenance costs more than offset the higher original costs.

Despite a steadily increasing demand, aluminium is a material which is unlikely to become in short supply, since there are large reserves of ore, well distributed over many countries. Processing these ores, however, demands large quantities of electricity, so that, in practice, those countries with cheap hydroelectric power are at a great advantage and production tends to be concentrated in these areas.

Asbestos

The fibrous mineral, asbestos, was being spun and woven into fire-resistant fabrics as early as 1870. To begin with, the fibres which were too short for spinning were treated as a waste product and thrown away, but in 1893 an Austrian textile manufacturer, Ludwig Hatschek, began experiments to mix them with a bonding agent to produce a new building material. After trying first bitumen and

29 The average size of the disc of glass made by the Old Crown glass process in which a blob of molten glass, after being gathered on the end of an open ended tube, was blown into a globe. By reheating and spinning the globe opened out by centrifugal force into a disc. Such a method only allowed very small sizes of usable glass

30 Sheet glass manufacture—the hand blown process. Opening the cylinder by attaching a hot piece of glass on the end

31 The casting hall at Pilkington Brothers Ravenhead glassworks, *c.* 1910. Only two bays now survive in their original condition and are scheduled for preservation

32 Polished plate manufacture—the old disc method of grinding and polishing. The photograph shows the method of fixing the plate in plaster of Paris on the disc table prior to grinding the surface

then magnesite, Hatschek succeeded, in 1900, in making the first asbestos-cement sheets. He adapted a Fourdrinier continuous paper-making machine for the purpose and fed it with a slurry containing 85 per cent cement and 15 per cent asbestos. Until 1908, when Millspaugh invented his vacuum method of extracting the water from either the paper pulp or the asbestos-cement slurry, there were great difficulties in drying the sheet. By 1910 asbestos-cement was being made in ten countries, including Britain.

In 1911 British Fibro-Cement, a subsidiary of a French company, began production at Erith, in Kent, and two years later Turner Brothers opened their asbestos-cement factory at Trafford Park, Manchester, to make flat sheets, 'Aegis Slates', and corrugated roofing slates, known as 'Trafford Tiles'. Some of the earliest Aegis Slates were used for roofing the Dunlop Cotton Mill at Castleton, near Rochdale. They are still in good condition. Trafford Tiles were used on a number of large contracts in the early 1920s, including the Empire Stadium at Wembley (1923). The 'Fibro Tile', made at Erith during the 1920s, was very similar to the 'Trafford Tile'. These corrugated sheets were considerably smaller than those in use today. They had only five corrugations, trodden into the soft sheet while it was lying on a corrugated template.

In 1917 a new factory was started in Widnes with Swiss capital and machines. New Swiss-built machinery was installed in 1923 and 1924 and this was used to make corrugated sheet, of the size and profile with which we are familiar today. The first asbestos-cement pipes were made at Widnes in 1927. Production was inefficient, however, until 1930, when a different type of Italian pipe-making machine was imported. By this time the Ministry of Health had approved asbestos-cement water-pipes, as an alternative to the traditional cast iron, and large quantities of the new pipes were sold to local authorities during the 1930s. They proved to have considerable advantages. Their resistance to corrosion is superior to that of iron and their jointing is flexible enough to absorb settlement or vibration without becoming loosened. Asbestos-cement sewer-pipes, first used in Britain in 1961, have had a similar success. So, too, have gutters and downpipes made in this material.

Asbestos-cement products are heavy and bulky in proportion to their value, so that transport costs have to be watched very carefully. For this reason, it has not been economic to centralise manufacture, in the way that the brickmakers have done. The pattern is one of a large number of factories, well distributed over Great Britain.

Bitumen and asphalt

Bitumen was valued as a waterproofing material in ancient Egypt, but it did not become extensively used in Europe until the nineteenth century, when improved methods of transport made it more practicable to import it from the major world source, the great Pitch Lake in Trinidad. It was shipped in hard blocks and used for pavements, cellar and basement flooring, flat-roofing and damp-courses, often combined with slate for this purpose. In the 1890s bituminous sheets became commercially available. These were made by running bitumen on to a strip of tough paper and were sold in large quantities for damp-coursing.

PATENT ASPHALTE ROOFING.

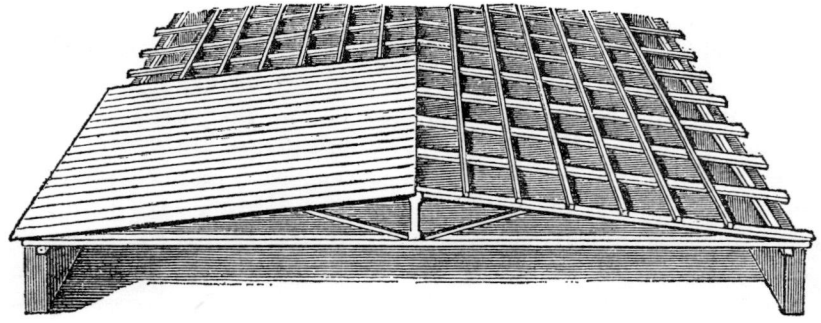

Figure 7 Patent asphalt roofing, 1844

Rock-asphalt became popular as a road-surfacing material during the second half of the nineteenth century. It is a fine-grained limestone, evenly impregnated with bitumen, in the proportion of about 10 per cent bitumen to 90 per cent limestone, and is found at a number of places in Europe, the chief of them being the Val de

Travers in Switzerland, Ragusa in Sicily and Limmer, near Hanover in Germany. It is obtained by mining, the seams varying in thickness between 6 and 10 feet, sandwiched between two layers of hard limestone.

At the works the lumps of rock are reduced to a fine powder, which is sold to customers either in its powdered state or as a mastic. The powder has been used mainly for road surfacing. It is heated, spread evenly over a concrete base and then compressed by men using iron rammers. Once it is laid constant traffic is needed in order to keep it compacted and it is consequently not suitable in this form for roofs or other building purposes.

The mastic is laid quite differently. It is prepared at the works by heating the powder with between 5 and 10 per cent of refined bitumen and then casting the thick liquid mixture into blocks. At the site where they are to be used, these blocks are broken up and heated in a cauldron for several hours, together with sand and a small quantity of bitumen. The asphalt is then run off into buckets and spread where it is required, with a wooden float. Properly laid, this produces an excellent waterproof coating. Poor results, which are unfortunately frequent, are usually caused either by not completing the work quickly and continuously, or by laying the mastic on a damp surface. The first type of carelessness causes cracks and the second blisters. If the asphalt is likely to be exposed to continuous periods of hot sunshine, as on a roof, then a higher proportion of sand has to be included in the mix.

Successful asphalting is very dependent on skilled, reliable workmen, which goes far to account for the indifferent reputation of presentday flat-roofing.

Plastics

Both the developed and the undeveloped industries have serious and growing housing problems. The solution to them must lie eventually in the creation of a new type of building industry, geared to industrial methods of production, and plastics can obviously play a large part in this development. In the meantime the market for plastics in building is already considerable. In Germany it is the biggest market of all and in Britain and the United States it is second only to the packaging market. The building industry's acceptance of plastics has been gradual, and we can expect to see a steady growth in the replacement of traditional methods, wherever technical and economic factors are in favour of plastics.

What builders call 'rainwater goods', guttering and downpipes, are an excellent case in point. Until the 1940s these were almost invariably of cast iron, although there had been some prewar experimenting with aluminium and asbestos-cement. The wartime shortage of metal provided a great encouragement to use alternative materials wherever possible and this, in practice, meant asbestos-cement. Military camps, hospitals, hostels and other priority buildings used asbestos-cement piping and guttering to take the rain away. Once the war was over plastic was increasingly used for this. The early examples were not well designed and the colours were unpleasing, but by the 1960s there had been great improvements and the market began to grow fast. Iron pipes and gutters are difficult to paint, so the work is often skimped, and they rust easily. Here was a case where the new material was bound to meet with a welcome, unless the price was impossibly high or the colour repulsive.

Plastic roofing panels also found ready customers, especially among industrialists. These panels and sheets were virtually unbreakable, they were light and easy to fix, and they could be made to exactly the same size and profile as sheets of corrugated asbestos-cement or aluminium. The initial disadvantage here was a tendency to yellow, but this fortunately belongs to the past.

Not all the technical disadvantages have yet been removed. Plastics are by their nature combustible and for some reason the building industry has shown itself more cautious about the combustibility of plastics than of other traditional materials, such as timber. In Britain the fire risk involved in the use of plastics is being investigated by the Rubber and Plastics Research Association, sponsored by the Building Group of the British Plastics Federation. The Association is also concerned with long-term research into a problem which worries builders and architects, the ability of plastics to withstand constant exposure to the weather.

So far, plastics are being used mainly in the finishing sectors of the building industry and the applications, where they occur, are largely all-plastic. The possibilities for plastics in structures are still untested, if not unexplored. Before structural plastics can become acceptable, there must be improvements in the properties of organic

SOME MAJOR NEW MATERIALS

polymers and there have already been suggestions as to how this might be accomplished.[2]

An increased use of plastics in building is also likely to come by combining them with other materials. Fully supported plastic sheet could make a perfectly adequate roof-covering and suitably reinforced plastic may within a few years provide a substitute for structural timber. Other applications of plastics which are in the experimental stage are for low-shrink rapid-setting cementless concrete and for acoustical insulation foam.

Plastics[3] constitute a whole group of materials as distinctive in their own way as the various types of wood and metal. These basic differences are widened even further by the fact that during the manufacturing process many plastics have their basic properties modified by the inclusion of substances such as plasticisers (which soften the material and make it more flexible), anti-oxidants (which help to prevent weakening under the influence of light or heat), fillers (which add a toughness not obtainable in the basic plastic) and colourants. Most plastics can be foamed, to produce lightweight materials.

With such a wide range of plastics now available, it is difficult to generalise about their properties, but, broadly speaking, plastics are light in weight, combustible, resistant to chemical action and adversely affected by sunlight, which can break down their colour and mechanical properties. They have a high strength to weight ratio, in some cases better than that of metal. They are much more flexible than other structural materials and for this reason they cannot be used as load-bearing structures in the conventional way. On the other hand, it has recently been proved that stressed skin plastics structures can be used to achieve remarkably strong buildings. A successful example of this is the use of sandwich panels made up of rigid foam between two skins of reinforced plastic.

Plastics, as chemical creations, unfortunately tend to have complicated names. Builders and merchants have tried to defend themselves against this by using the trade name as the generic term for the material. Bakelite for phenolics, for example, and Perspex for acrylics. This has resulted in a curious mixture of scientific and popular labels, not easy to avoid. Nevertheless the main types of plastic and the uses which the building industry makes of them can be briefly described without a great deal of misunderstanding.

The decorative laminates. These are supplied either as a veneer or with the veneer ready bonded to a wide range of core materials, such as hardboard, particle board and plasterboard. The standard $\frac{1}{16}$th inch decorative laminated veneer is a hard, dense material, made by subjecting a number of layers of paper impregnated with synthetic resin to heat and pressure. Decorative laminates are extremely durable materials. They are sold under such trade names as Formica, Arborite, Warerite and Perstorp.

Epoxide Resins. These are used in adhesives, concrete repair compositions, surface coatings and for making reinforced plastics. Before use, they have to be mixed with hardeners. The hardened resins are tough and stable, with excellent mechanical and electrical properties and good chemical resistance. They adhere strongly to metal, concrete, timber, ceramics and glass.

Melamine Formaldehyde. Melamine is supplied in the form of mouldings and as a liquid resin for the surfacing of decorative laminates.

Nylon. This is a general name for a whole family of thermoplastic materials, more correctly called polyamides. Nylon is tough, strong and abrasion-resistant. It is widely used for making building components, such as window fittings, castors and door furniture, which have to withstand friction.

Phenol Formaldehyde. These materials, also known as Phenolic and Bakelite, were the first true plastics. They are used, with suitable fillers, as moulding materials to make, for instance, lavatory seats and electrical fittings. The fillers can be paper, sawdust, nylon, asbestos, cotton or glass-fibre, according to the type and quality of product required. Sunlight causes phenolics to lose their colour and they are consequently produced only in the darker colours.

Polystyrene. Polystyrene is a cheap material, which can be moulded to produce a good surface finish. Its properties are much improved by blending it with synthetic rubber. It is used for sheet—much in favour for shuttering—mouldings, such as lavatory cisterns and wall-tiles, and as a cellular material. In the form of expanded polystyrene, which is 98 per cent air, this is one of the best and cheapest insulating materials, supplied in sheets, boards or mouldings.

SOME MAJOR NEW MATERIALS 91

Polythene (Polyethylene). This is a very versatile plastic, available in three forms, film or sheet, mouldings and extrusions. The film is used for damp-courses, onsite protection of men, materials and machinery, and for curing concrete. The mouldings and extrusions include cisterns, cold-water pipes and pipe fittings.

Polyvinyl Chloride (PVC, Vinyl). PVC can be compounded with plasticisers and fillers to provide a remarkable range of flexibility, from rubberlike to tough and rigid. The range of applications covers roof light sheeting, rainwater goods, wall tiles, floor coverings and handrail coverings. The cladding of industrial buildings with PVC coated metals has become widely accepted.

Polyvinyl Fluoride (PVF, Tedlan). This is supplied as a film which can be bonded or laminated to a variety of materials, galvanised steel, asbestos board and plywood being only a few. It gives a hard stain-resistant surface.

Reinforced Plastics (GRP, polyester glass, fibre glass). The term 'reinforced plastics' can be applied to any type of plastic material containing a reinforcing agent, but it has been reserved recently for mouldings produced from glass fibre and either polyester or epoxide resins. These mouldings are strong and particularly useful in the casting of elaborate concrete shapes.

Urea Formaldehyde. This is used for door and cabinet fittings, for bonding plywood and for making a cellular insulating material that can be foamed within wall cavities.

It seems likely that the future pattern of development for plastics in building will tend increasingly towards structural applications, as well as to non-load-bearing uses. One factor which is very much in their favour is that, in contrast to all other constructional materials, the prices of plastics are steadily dropping.

Plasterboard

Plasterboard, perhaps better called plaster panels, consists of gypsum plaster sandwiches between two sheets of paper. It originated in the United States.[4] Augustus Sackett's first patent was taken out in New York in 1894 and by 1910 this very useful material was being widely used in America. It did not become popular in Britain until the mid

1920s, largely because of trade union opposition. There were two solid reasons for its earlier acceptance in the United States. With the serious shortage of skilled plasterers there, it allowed plastering work to be carried out much quicker, and, in timber houses it provided a much-needed fire-retarding lining for highly inflammable walls and ceilings.

Between 1934 and 1939 plasterboard was increasingly used by speculative builders as a substitute for lath and plaster. During the war it was one of the very few building materials to be in good supply and it was widely used for repairing bomb-damaged premises and for lining huts. In the immediate postwar years it was an indispensable component of a large proportion of both temporary and permanent houses.

Since its original invention, plasterboard has been greatly improved and developed, especially during the past twenty-five years. One of the earliest improvements was to cover one side of the board with a type of paper that would either hold a thin coat of plaster, skimmed all over the wall or ceiling, so as to give a jointless surface, or could be finished with a coat of paint or distemper. If the painted finish was chosen, the joints had first to be taped or filled with plaster. Other recent techniques have been to fix plasterboard directly to brick or concrete block walls by means of adhesives or screws and, by using boards with recessed or tapered edges, to leave the joints unfilled as a decorative feature or to fill them without needing a skim-coat over the whole wall.

The poor thermal insulation of the original plasterboard has been largely overcome by making the board with a facing of aluminium foil on one side. The first time this type of board was used in Britain was in 1949, when the Ministry of Works built ninety-four semi-detached and terraced houses in Canterbury for the War Office, as married quarters. The system was also used in 1952–54, when the National Coal Board built several hundred houses in Staffordshire. The plaster panels were cast in small temporary factories near the sites, but, largely because of poor organisation many of the panels were damaged during transport and erection, and a good deal of subsequent patching was needed.

In 1947 a new type of panel was pioneered at the Sound City film studios at Shepperton, in Middlesex. A complete prototype house was built here of cast plaster panels, consisting of two plaster faces separated by a honeycomb core. These eventually became the well-known Bellrock plaster panels, which are now widely used for partitions and wall-linings, 3, 4 and 6 inches thick. In some cases these have been used for load-bearing partitions and for the inner skin of cavity walls.

During the 1950s the manufacturers began to market plasterboard partition units, made up of two layers of plasterboard enclosing a honeycomb core of coated cardboard. Plasterboards are also made for partition units as room-high planks, 2 feet wide and $\frac{3}{4}$ inch thick, to fit into aluminium runners on the floor and ceiling.

Plasterboard is a very useful building material. Its one serious defect is that it is a poor insulator against noise, as many inhabitants of postwar flats have found to their cost.

APPENDIX ONE

The Development of Building Regulations

The first attempt to control building in London dates from 1189, when it was laid down at FitzAlwyn's Assize that all party walls were to be of stone or brick, as a precaution against the spread of fire. This regulation remained in force until the mid-seventeenth century, but it was only very partially observed. In London, as in other English towns, the houses were generally constructed of timber frames, on a stone or brick foundation, with the spaces between the framing-timbers filled in with lath and plaster. The storeys projected one above the other, to give additional protection from the weather. In this way, the top floors on either side of the street were brought very close together and the fire risk was greatly increased. During the early part of the seventeenth century there were attempts to encourage the use of brick and many new houses and public buildings were of this material, but at the time of the Great Fire in 1666 most of the buildings within the City of London were still of the timber and lath-and-plaster type.

After the destruction caused by the Great Fire Parliament passed 'An Act for the rebuilding of the City of London'. It gave London a complete code of building regulations. 'For better regulations, uniformity and gracefulness', only four types of house were allowed in the City.

The first and least distinguished sort were to be built in by-lanes, two storeys high, not counting cellars and garrets. The second, 'in streets and lanes of note' were to be three storeys high. The third, fronting 'high and principal streets', were of four storeys. The fourth, the merchants' houses 'of the greatest bigness', were also not to exceed four storeys.

The hard and fast division of streets into these categories was eventually found to be impracticable and only six streets were in fact classed as 'high and principal streets', in which only houses of four storeys were permitted. For each type of house, there were precise regulations as to the thickness of walls, heights of ceilings, timber sizes and other details. There were sharp penalties for defaulters, including imprisonment, and the authorities were given powers to demolish any building which failed to meet the regulations.

The 1667 Act contained an important clause dealing with foundations. When the trenches were dug, ready for the footings to be laid, the builder had to notify the City Surveyor, who then inspected them. A fee of 6s 8d was payable for this service.

Another clause was concerned with party walls. They had to be of brick or stone, and a minimum of 14 inches thick, except in the attics, where 9 inches was permitted.

Since the pioneering 1667 Act there have been many modifications to cover new materials, techniques and social conditions. Throughout the eighteenth and nineteenth centuries, the London Building Acts provided a model not only for other English cities, but for other countries. The New York Building Code, for instance, owed a good deal to London's long experience in these matters.

The basic thinking throughout the eighteenth century was that there should be certain minimum standards for all buildings, but that above that some elasticity was necessary, to meet the needs and budgets of different kinds of owner. The Act passed in the first year of Queen Anne's reign illustrates this principle, and also shows how the minimum standards were being continually raised in the light of experience. Party walls now had to be 18 inches thick—14 inches in the attics—and they had to be carried 18 inches above the level at which the roof began. No timber was to be let into any section of the party wall. These provisions applied to all houses, but the regulations concerning the thickness of front and rear walls were more flexible. Houses 'of first rate of building' had to observe a minimum thickness of 18 inches for the cellars, 14 inches for the next two floors and 9 inches for the garrets. For the 'second-rate of building' the figures were $22\frac{1}{2}$ inches for the cellars, 18 inches for the next two floors, 14 inches for the third floor and 9 inches for the garrets. For the 'third rate of building' it was 27 inches for the cellars, $22\frac{1}{2}$ inches for the first floor, 14 inches for the next three floors and 9 inches for the garrets. 'The fourth rate of building, being chiefly for Noblemen, may have their thickness left to the Discretion of the Architect.'

By the end of the nineteenth century every aspect of the construction of a building was tightly controlled. The 1894 Act consolidated, extended and brought up to date the regulations which had governed the huge expansion and rebuilding of London during the Victorian period. This was the framework within which British builders had to work and within which the suppliers of material had to carry on business. The regulations were getting tougher all the time. The Act itself, for instance, specified that 'the footings of a wall shall rest upon the solid ground or concrete or upon other solid substructure', but an amendment, passed only two years later, said: 'The foundations of the walls of every house or building shall be formed of a bed of good concrete not less than 9 inches thick and projecting at least 4 inches on each side of the lowest course of footings.' The amendment was, of course, greatly welcomed by the cement manufacturers and quarry owners, since it involved an automatic growth of their market. The brickmakers had equal reason to bless the Building Act, which prescribed that:

> 'the projection of the bottom of the footings of every wall on each side of the wall shall be at least equal to half of the thickness of the wall at its base, unless an adjoining wall interferes, in which case the projection may be omitted where that wall adjoins, and the diminution of the footings of every wall shall be formed in regular offsets and the height from the bottom of such footing to the base of the wall shall be at least equal to two-thirds of the thickness of the wall at its base.'

This meant that, in the case of a $13\frac{1}{2}$ inch wall, the height of the footings would have to be 9 inches, or three courses of brickwork.

Above ground the standards of brickwork were equally firmly controlled. In the case of factory chimneys, for instance, the brickwork at the top had to be 9 inches thick, increasing half a brick in thickness for every 20 feet downwards.

> The shaft shall taper gradually from the base to the top at the rate of at least $2\frac{1}{2}$ inches in 10 feet of height. The width of the base of the shaft of square shall be at least one-tenth of the proposed height of the shaft, or if round or any other shape, then one-

twelfth of the height. Firebricks built inside the lower portion of the shaft shall be provided, as additional to and independent of the prescribed thickness of brickwork, and shall not be bonded therewith.

The same Act and its amendments ordered that every roof or roof structure in the London district should be covered with slate, tile, metal or other incombustible material. No roof was to be covered with thatch, or other inflammable material. The pitch of the roofs of warehouse buildings must not be greater than 47 per cent and in the case of other buildings 75 per cent. The framing of roofs of more than 60° pitch on a building more than 45 feet in height had to be of fireproof material at least two inches thick.

Local authorities throughout Britain came to use the London Building Act as a model for their own bye-laws and both were conservative. In 1912 the Local Government Board sent a circular to District Councils, asking whether their building bye-laws, made under the Public Health Act of 1875, were appropriate to new forms of construction and new building materials. The implication was that these bye-laws were out of date and needed revising, which was certainly true. The thicknesses required for ordinary brick walls, for instance, were not appropriate to walls made of concrete or hollow blocks. A Departmental Committee was appointed in 1914 to look into this problem, but, as a result of the war, it was unable to issue its report until 1918. This revealed a very unsatisfactory state of affairs. One builder told the Committee of one case in which 6 inches of concrete had been insisted on where 3 inches of sand would have been just as effective and of another where rock, gravel and chalk had to be removed in order to substitute concrete, which was not as strong as the material taken away.

The ultimate in absurdity was reached by the controls exercised over the Ritz Hotel (1904), the first completely steel-framed building in London. The load was completely taken by steel columns, but the architect was compelled as a result of the bye-laws to make the external walls of full load-bearing thickness and strength, even though they carried no load at all.

APPENDIX TWO

Key Dates

1773	Plate glass first manufactured in England
1774	Coade stone first made
	London Building Act
	Bramah's water-closet
1779	Iron Bridge, Coalbrookdale
1784	Brick Tax introduced
1786	Reed's patent for a nailmaking machine
1795	Strutt's Mill at Belper
1796	Parker's patent for a 'Roman' cement
1797	Bage's Mill, Shrewsbury
1810	Kennet and Avon Canal—increased market for Bath stone
1815	Cast-iron staircases, Brighton Pavilion
	Doulton's Lambeth Pottery
1824	Aspdin's patent for Portland cement
1834	Institute of British Architects
1836	Godwin's *Nature and Properties of Concrete*
1839	Report on building stones for the House of Commons
c. 1840	First plywood
1841	Patent for wire-cut bricks
1842	Chadwick's Report to the Poor Law Commissioners
1844	Metropolitan Building Act
	Prefabricated iron houses exported to Africa
1845	Burton's Palm House at Kew
	Glass duty abolished
	Public Health Act
1850	Brick tax removed
	Rolled-iron sections become available
1851	Crystal Palace
1854	Wilkinson's patent for reinforced concrete beams
1855	Brunel's prefabricated hospital in the Crimea

APPENDIX TWO

1857	Invention of concrete-mixer
1858	Local Government Acts or bye-laws and loans for housing
1859	Sheerness Boat Store
	First glazed kitchen sink
1862	Hoffmann continuous kiln for brickmaking
1864	First tenements built by Peabody Trust
1875	First machine for extruding bricks
1877	Crompton's rotary kiln for cement
c. 1890	Knife cutting machine for veneers
	Fletton process for brickmaking
	Metal extrusion process introduced
1894	Sackett's first patent for plasterboard
1897	Aluminium covering for dome of San Giacchino, Rome
1900	Glass bricks become available
	First asbestos-cement sheets
	'Glass-silk' made in Germany
1904	Ritz Hotel, first steel-framed building in London
	Millboard made in Britain
1910	First glass and concrete rooflights in Britain, on Whiteley's and at Kodak factory
1917	Plasterboard first used in England
1920	First standard steel windows in Britain
1923	Corrugated asbestos made in Britain
1933	Aluminium windows
1936	Peter Jones' store, London—curtain walling
1945	Aluminium bungalows

References

CHAPTER ONE *Builders and Customers*, 1770–1970

1. On this see Henry-Russell Hitchcock, *Early Victorian Architecture in Britain*, Architectural Press, 1954, vol. i, p. 436.
2. Some of this evidence is contained in Appendix XV of *Housing of the Working Classes*, 1855–1912, published by the London County Council in 1913.
3. *Pamphlets on Reconstruction Problems*, vol. i, Pamphlet no. 2, *Housing in England and Wales*, 1917.
4. *Ibid.*
5. On their export trade in iron buildings, see Hitchcock, *op. cit.*, vol. i, Chapter 7.
6. 7 January 1860.
7. See F. Jenkins, *Architect and Patron*, Oxford University Press, 1961, pp. 199–201.
8. Hitchcock, *op. cit.*, vol. i, p. 477.

CHAPTER TWO *Stone and Slate*

1. For a general description of British building stones, see B. C. G. Shore, *The Stones of Britain*, Hill, 1957.
2. The techniques of quarrying and dressing Cornish granite are described in Helen Harris, *Industrial Archaeology of Dartmoor*, David & Charles, 1968, pp. 70–7.
3. M. Davies-Shiel and J. D. Marshall, *Industrial Archaeology of the Lake Counties*, David & Charles, 1969, pp. 157–8.
4. Details of the history and archaeology of the Scottish granite industry are given in John Butt, *Industrial Archaeology of Scotland*, David & Charles, 1967, pp. 98–9.
5. See Kenneth Hudson, *The Fashionable Stone*, Adam & Dart, 1971, p. 33.

REFERENCES

6   *The New Practical Builder*, 1823, p. 286.
7   *Essay Towards a Description of Bath*, 1749, p. 33.

CHAPTER THREE *Bricks and Tiles*

1   N. Davey, *A History of Building Materials*, Phoenix House, 1961, p. 78.
2   David Smith, *The Industrial Archaeology of the East Midlands*, David & Charles, p. 141.
3   Quoted in Martin S. Briggs, *A Short History of the Building Crafts*, Oxford University Press, 1925, p. 113.
4   See also S. B. Hamilton, 'Coade Stone', *Architectural Review*, November 1954.
5   D. Eyles, *Royal Doulton, 1815–1965*, Hutchinson, 1965.
6   Sir Edwin Chadwick, *The Sanitary Condition of the Labouring Population*, H.M.S.O., Sessional Paper, vol. 26, 1842.

CHAPTER FOUR *Lime, Cement, Plaster and Concrete*

1   On the processing of gypsum and on the various proprietary plasters made from it, see Davey, *A History of Building Materials*, Phoenix House, pp. 92–6.
2   Examples of the stucco from Nonesuch can be seen at the Victoria and Albert Museum.
3   Davey, p. 117.
4   After Pozzuoli in Italy, where a natural source of such material exists, in the form of volcanic earth.
5   Details of these tests are given by A. W. Skempton, 'Portland Cement, 1843–87', *Trans. Newcomen Soc.*, vol. xxxv, 1962–63.
6   Since *c.* 1880, many specialised types of cement have been produced. At the end of the nineteenth century it was found that granulated blast-furnace slag could be usefully added to the Portland cement clinker, provided it was rapidly cooled after having been discharged from the furnace. This type of cement is known as Portland blast-furnace cement. It contains up to 65 per cent of granulated slag.
   A very rapid-hardening cement was first produced in France in 1908 and patented under the name 'cement-fondu'. It is made, at a high temperature, by melting a mixture of limestone and bauxite.

7 J. M. Crook, 'Sir Robert Smirke: a Pioneer of Concrete Construction', *Trans. Newcomen Soc.*, vol. xxxviii, 1965–66.
8 A full description is given in Joyce M. Brown, 'W. B. Wilkinson, 1819–1902, and his place in the history of reinforced concrete.' *Trans. Newcomen Soc.*, vol. xxxix, 1966–67.
9 *Ibid.*
10 The history and the technology of no-fines concrete are discussed in 'No-fines concrete as a structural material', *Proc. Inst. Civil Engineers*, vol. v, November 1956.
11 *A Work Study in Blocklaying*, National Building Studies Technical Paper, 1948.
12 R. B. White, *Prefabrication: A History of its Development in Great Britain*, H.M.S.O., 1965, p. 14.

CHAPTER FIVE *Glass, Iron and Steel*
1 T. C. Barker, *Pilkington Brothers and the Glass Industry*, Allen & Unwin, 1960, p. 63.
2 For additional details see *ibid.*, p. 83.
3 Paxton's negotiations with the glass-makers are described in G. F. Chadwick, *The Work of Sir Joseph Paxton*, Architectural Press, 1961, and in Barker, *op. cit.*
4 Morton Shand. See also Henry-Russell Hitchcock, *Architecture in the Nineteenth and Twentieth Centuries*, Chapter 7. A good short account of the use of iron in building during the nineteenth century, with an interesting range of continental examples in Heinrich Wurm, *Vorgefertigte Bauwerke des 19 Jahrhunderts*, 1966, published by the Association of German Engineers.
5 By R. J. M. Sutherland, 'The Introduction of Structural Wrought Iron', *Trans. Newcomen Soc.*, vol. xxxvi, 1963–64.
6 John Gloag and Derek Bridgwater, *A History of Cast Iron in Architecture*, Allen & Unwin, 1948.

CHAPTER SIX *Timber, Plywood and Wood Products*
1 On the history of screws, see H. W. Dickinson, 'The Origin and Manufacture of Wood Screws', *Trans. Newcomen Soc.*, vol. xxii, 1941–42, pp. 79–89. The Wyatts' achievement is placed in its

machine-building context by L. T. C. Rolt, *Tools for the Job*, 1965, Batsford, 1965, pp. 58–9.
2   See L. T. C. Rolt, *Isambard Kingdom Brunel*, Longmans, 1957, pp. 175–9.
3   *Ibid.*, p. 177.
4   Beckman, *History of Inventions*, 1830, p. 376.
5   'Five laminated timber arches for an archway to the festival', *Wood*, 1950, no. 15, pp. 398–403.
6   W. T. Curry, 'Laminated versus solid timber beams', *Wood*, 1955, no. 20, pp. 386–8.
7   For details of the original manufacturing process and of the later improvements, see M. Bowley, *Innovations in Building Materials*, Duckworth, 1960.

CHAPTER SEVEN *Some Major New Materials*
1   'Aluminium' normally means one of the many aluminium alloys. Winifred Lewis, *The Light Metals Industry*, Temple Press, (1949) lists 141 of these, all commercially available.
2   H. F. Mark, *Plastics and Polymers*, February 1969.
3   For a detailed account of the applications of plastics to building, see P. Reboul and R. G. Bruce Mitchell, *Plastics in the Building Industry*, Newnes, 1960.
4   'The History of Plasterboard', *The Gypsum Journal*, April, June, September 1958.

Notes to Plates and Line Drawings

Plate 23
The Iron Palace of King Eyambo, 'one of the African princes on the Calabar river, built by Mr Wm Laycock, iron merchant, of Oldhall-Street'.

Plate 24
Iron House for Châgres, made by Mr Walker of Mill Wall, Poplar, commissioned by the Royal Mail Steam Packet Company for their Superintendent and other officers at the port. 'At the present moment Mr Walker's factory presents rather a busy scene, for, in addition to the above, he had in course of construction 36 iron houses for the residences of emigrants sent out by Government to Australia. The factory itself occupies a space of about three acres, on which over 400 men are continually employed at a weekly expenditure of about £800.'

Figure 4
Hatcher's Benenden tile machine. 'The above machine may be seen at Work daily from Twelve to Three o'Clock, at Cottam & Hallen's, No. 2 Winsley-street, Oxford-street. This machine will make 11,000 feet of good Drain Tiles per day, with only two small boys, one large boy, and one man, to work it; it will make tiles of any shape, or perfectly cylindrical as pipes. No patent dues or licence charged on the articles made; the purchase of the Machine includes free use of it.'

Figure 7
Patent asphalt roofing. 'The above material has been used and approved by the Nobility, Gentry, and Agriculturists generally, as a Roofing and Covering to sides of farm buildings; its advantages are—Lightness, Durability and Economy. Being a non-conductor, it has been proved an efficient "Protective Material" to Plants, and is now in use at the "Royal Horticultural Society's Gardens, Chiswick". It can be had of any length, 32 inches wide, at One Penny per superficial foot.'

Gazetteer

Any town or village is a museum of building and it is a matter of personal curiosity and observation to discover the materials and standards of construction which have been used at different periods. The ideal laboratory for the archaeology and history of building material is, unfortunately, a demolition site, where the techniques of yesterday's builders are laid bare.

The examples which follow are merely an indication of the kind of evidence to look for, so far as the traditional methods are concerned. They in no way represent a comprehensive list. Instances of the use of the more recent materials, such as plastics and asbestos, are not included.

CHAPTER ONE: *Builders and Customers, 1770–1970*

Bournville, Birmingham. From 1895. One of the most celebrated of the garden cities, built by Cadbury's. The contrast with other workers' housing in Birmingham is marked now and was even more so in the late nineteenth century.

Cronkbourne Village, Kirk Braddon, Isle of Man. 1846–50. A model estate of forty-two houses, in two parallel terraces, built for the workers in the local sail-cloth factory. The first community in the island to have electric light.

New Lanark. An industrial community, with housing and public buildings commissioned by Robert Owen, from 1799 onwards. Subsequently modernised.

Port Sunlight, Cheshire. The earliest of the garden cities, built by a major industrial concern, Lever Brothers, later Unilever, to give workers a standard of housing hitherto thought appropriate only to the middle classes. 1888 onwards.

Swindon. The Railway Village in New Town, near the railway works, built during the 1840s to house employees of the Company.

CHAPTER TWO: *Stone and Slate*

Bath, Combe Down. Ralph Allen's quarry here has been built over, but the face of the cliff into which the mines ran can be seen at the back of a house called 'The Firs'.

Bath, Somerset. Prior Park, Ralph Allen's own seat and show house, built to demonstrate what could be done with Bath stone, properly selected and expertly handled.

Box, Wiltshire. Hazlebury quarry. In use from the seventh century (Saxon church of St Laurence, Bradford-on-Avon) to the seventeenth. One of the most important sources of limestone of the Bath stone type.

Chilmark, Wiltshire. This limestone quarry, near Salisbury, was used for the cathedrals at Old Sarum and Salisbury, and for many of the Norman churches in south Wiltshire and north Dorset.

Clipsham, Rutland. These famous limestone quarries, still in use, have been worked since the fourteenth century. They have supplied the stone for many churches, cathedrals and public buildings and for refacing a number of the Oxford and Cambridge colleges.

Corsham, Wiltshire. Stone mines, Monks Park, which is still in operation, extracts the freestone at about 200 feet below the surface.

Giffnay, Renfrewshire. The quarries here provided much of the sandstone for the Victorian expansion of Glasgow.

Haslingden, Lancashire. Extensive remains of nineteenth-century sandstone quarrying. The quarries in Haslingden, Rawtenstall, Bacup and Whitworth provided much of the stone for building the east Lancashire towns. Haslingden stone was used throughout the country and was also exported.

Haytor, Islington, Devon. The most famous of the Dartmoor granite quarries, opened in 1820 and long derelict.

Kemnay, Aberdeenshire. Here and at Rubislaw were the most important granite quarries in Aberdeenshire. Paradise Hill quarry is still in use.

London, Oxford Street. Selfridge's store, built in the early 1920s, was one of several major buildings erected during the 1920s for which Portland stone was used as a facing.

London, Westminster. The Banqueting House, Whitehall (1622). Designed by Inigo Jones, it was one of the earliest buildings in London to use Portland stone and marked the beginning of a fashion in this respect.

Merrivale, Devon. Tor Quarry, one of the most productive on Dartmoor. Opened in 1876 and still functioning.
Montacute, Somerset. Montacute House, begun in 1590, was built of the yellow-brown limestone from the nearby quarries at Ham Hill, which have been worked since Roman times.
Portland, Dorset. After more than four centuries of extensive exploitation, the island is pitted with quarries, many of them deep.
Shap, Westmorland. Granite quarries, started in 1864. The 'Blue' quarry is $\frac{1}{4}$ mile north of the turning to the Shap Wells Hotel and the 'Pink' quarry is about $2\frac{1}{2}$ miles farther south.

CHAPTER THREE: *Bricks and tiles*

Ashburnham, Sussex. The Ashburnham Estate brickworks. This was probably the last brickworks in Britain to make bricks by entirely traditional methods. It began production in 1840 and closed in 1968.
Bristol, Bedminster. A number of the larger commercial buildings here, including Wills tobacco factory and some of the bonded warehouses, were built 1890–1910 with the local Cattybrook bricks, easily recognised by their harsh red colour. The brickworks itself, not far from the entrance to the Severn railway tunnel, is still in operation.
Bristol. J. L. and E. Pearce's Warehouse, 1869, in Welsh Back. Designed by Ponton and Gough in an ornate Florentine style. Excellent brickwork, with impressive detailing.
Broxbourne, Hertfordshire. Remains of James Pulham's celebrated terra cotta and artificial stone works (1846–1940) which held a Royal Warrant of Appointment to Edward VII and George V. Most of the premises have been demolished to make room for a car park, but parts remain, including a kiln.
Dorchester, Dorset. Eldridge Pope's brewery, 1870–72. Designed by Crickenay in Victorian polychromatic style, using different kinds of local bricks.
Glencaise, Perthshire. Remains of the Pitfour brickworks, important in the nineteenth century. The grassed-over Hoffmann kiln, 1871, can still be seen.
London, Westminster. Coade Stone lion, 1837, at south end of Westminster Bridge. The symbol of the Lion Brewery, formerly on the South Bank. One of the last products of the Coade Artificial Stone Works, which were situated nearby in Belvedere Road.

Measham, Leicestershire. Site of brickworks, between the Leicester Road and Bosworth Road, where Joseph Wilkes made his famous large-size bricks, 'Wilkes' Gobs'. Some of these bricks can be seen in a row of cottages known as The Brickyards and in other walls and houses in the town.
Stewartby, Bedfordshire. A brickmaking village, adjoining the great Fletton brickworks. Begun in 1926.
Swadlincote, Derbyshire. An important refractory and stoneware-producing region, with three firms that have been in business since 1810. One, T. G. Green and Co., still has a number of bottle-kilns, two of them more than 100 years old.
Ware, Hertfordshire. Houses, including Nos. 99–105 and the Rose and Crown in Walton Road, and boundary walls containing bricks 12 by 6 by 6 inches patented by Caleb Hitch, of Ware. These bricks had interlocking flanges and cavities, to economise in mortar and increase structural strength.

CHAPTER FOUR: *Lime, cement, plaster and concrete*

Brent, Middlesex. Quainton, Verney, Alyesbury and Chesham Streets. Metropolitan Railway housing estate, 1880–1925. The original estate of 140 brick-built houses was much extended in 1925 by the addition of semi-detached houses built by industrialised methods, using precast concrete sections.
Bromley, Kent. Anerley New Church, 1881, Waldegrave Road. Pink, rough mass concrete construction by W. J. E. Henley.
Buxton, Derbyshire. One of many lime-producing centres in the county, with large-scale activity since the 1780s. There are extensive workings and waste heaps to the north and south-west of the town. There is a large kiln at the Perseverance Works, Dove Holes. The Harpur Hill works of the Buxton Lime Firms had a Hoffmann kiln, operating from 1872 to 1947, which was one of the largest in Britain.
Kendal, Westmorland. Extensive lime-burning took place on Kendal Fell, on the western outskirts of the town, from 1820 onwards. There is a double-hearth kiln on the north side of the Underbarrow road.
Lynmouth, Devon. A group of mid-eighteenth-century limekilns built into the cliff along the promenade has been converted into a shelter for holidaymakers. The lime was brought by sea from South

Wales. A number of these kilns can still be seen on the north Devon coast, from Glenthorne to Hartland.
Wembley, Middlesex. Empire Pool, 1934. At the time it was completed it had the largest clear span in reinforced concrete in the world, 220 feet.

CHAPTER FIVE: *Glass, iron and steel*

Glasgow. Gardner's store, 1856, Jamaica Street, by James Baird. The whole front of this building was constructed in glass and cast iron.
Hampton Court Palace. The East and South fronts, built by Wren, 1689–1702, have the original glazing, which shows in the slight curvature and brilliant fire-finish of crown glass.
Kew, Palm House. Designed by Decimus Burton and Richard Turner, 1844–46. With the destruction of the Crystal Palace and the Chatsworth Conservatory, this is the most notable survival of the early glass and iron structures built for horticultural purposes.
London, Isleworth. Syon House. Elegant glasshouse, 1827–30, by Charles Fowler, with excellent use of glass and cast iron in the roof and dome. Now the Syon Garden Centre.
London, Peter Jones store, Sloane Square. Designed by Slater and Moberley, 1936. An interesting precursor of the glass curtain-wall technique, with concrete breastwork acting as mullions.
London, Piccadilly. Ritz Hotel (1904). The first completely steel-framed building in London.
London, Royal Opera Arcade. Designed by M. Novosielski, 1790. The glazed lanterns provide top light and the individual shop fronts have curved glass at the sides.
London, West Ham Abbey Mills Sewage Pumping Station. Built by the Metropolitan Board of Works, 1865–68. Contains remarkable interior cast iron work.
St Helens, Lancashire. At Pilkington's Ravenhead glassworks two bays of the original casting hall, 1773, still survive. In the walls are traces of what may have been annealing furnaces. Pilkingtons Museum of Glass shows the development of the industry from its earliest days.
Sheerness, Kent. The Boat Store (1859) in the dockyard. Cast iron frame, with glass and corrugated iron panel infitting. Iron roof trusses. Designed by Col. G. T. Greene.

Stonehouse Gloucestershire. Stanley Mill, 1813. A very beautiful cloth mill, built of brick and stone, with double iron pillars supporting the iron floor beams. The mill is fire-proof, the floors consisting of brick arches resting on the iron beams, with stone paving laid on top of the arches.

CHAPTER SIX: *Timber, plywood and wooden products*

Alton, Hampshire. Crowley's Brewery. The maltings are older than the other buildings and may date from 1790. The northern maltings are remarkable for their cathedral-sized roof, with its ingenious and well-preserved timber structure.

Bradford, Yorkshire. Mills occupied by James Drummond and Sons, Lumb Lane. Laminated roof construction in a worsted mill built *c.* 1895. The laminations are 5 inches by 1 inch deal, nailed and bolted together to form an overall span of 40 feet.

London, Chiswell Street, E.C.1. The Porter Tun Room in Whitbread's Brewery, built in 1773, has a timber roof with a clear span of 65 feet, second only to Westminster Hall.

York. In York Railway Museum there is part of the arch of a bridge, made in laminated timber, made by J. and B. Green, and in service from 1839 until 1937.

Select Bibliography

GENERAL WORKS ON THE HISTORY OF BUILDING AND BUILDING MATERIALS

BOWLEY, M. *Innovations in Building Materials*, Duckworth, 1960
BRIGGS, M. S. *A Short History of the Building Crafts*, Oxford University Press, 1925
BRUNSKILL, R. W. *Illustrated Handbook of Vernacular Architecture*, Faber, 1971
CHAPMAN, STANLEY D. *The History of Working Class Housing*, David & Charles, 1971
CLIFTON-TAYLOR, A. *The Pattern of English Building*, 2nd edn, Batsford, 1925
DAVEY, N. *A History of Building Materials*, Phoenix House, 1961
DE MARÉ, E. *New Ways of Building*, 3rd edn, Architectural Press, 1958
DE MARÉ, E. *The Functional Tradition in Early Industrial Buildings*, 1958
HAMILTON, S. B. *A Short History of the Structural Fire Protection of Buildings*, H.M.S.O. for Building Research Station, 1958
HITCHCOCK, H. R. *Architecture: Nineteenth and Twentieth Centuries*, 3rd edn, Pelican History of Art, 1969
HITCHCOCK, H. R. *Early Victorian Architecture in Britain*, Architectural Press, 1954
INNOCENT, C. F. *The Development of English Building Construction*, 1916, reprint edn, 1971
KNIGHT, B. H. AND KNIGHT, R. G. *Builders' Materials*, 3rd edn, Edward Arnold, 1955
MADGE, J. *Tomorrow's Houses: new building methods, structures and materials*, Pilot Press, 1946
MIDDLETON, G. A. T. *Building Materials*, 1909
MOXON, J. *Mechanick Exercises*, 1678

RHODES, DANIEL. *Kilns: Design, Construction and Operation*, Pitman, 1968
SALZMAN, L. F. *Building in England down to 1540*, Oxford University Press, 1952
TIMOSHENKO, S. P. *History of Strength of Materials*, McGraw Hill, 1953
WHITE, R. B. *Prefabrication: a history of its development in Great Britain*, H.M.S.O., 1965
WILLIAMS, A. J. *Building and Builders*, Longmans, 1968

Bricks and Tiles

BEDFORDSHIRE COUNTY PLANNING DEPARTMENT. *Bedfordshire Brickfield*, 1967
BUTTERWORTH, B. *Bricks and Modern Research*, Lockwood, 1948
DOBSON, E. *Bricks and Tiles*, 1890
LLOYD, N. *A History of English Brickwork*, H. G. Montgomery, 1928
LESLIE, KIM C. 'The Ashburnham Estate Brickworks, 1840–1968', *Sussex Industrial History*, Winter 1970–71
YOUNG, D. 'Brickmaking at Sandleheath, Hampshire', *Industrial Archaeology*, November 1960

Cement and Concrete

BILL, MAX. *Robert Maillart—Bridges and Constructions*, trans. from German, 3rd edn, Pall Mall Press, 1969
BROWN, J. M. 'W. B. Wilkinson (1819–1902) and his place in the history of reinforced concrete', *Trans. Newcomen Soc.*, vol. xxxix, 1966–67.
COLLINS, P. *Concrete: the visions of a new architecture*, Faber, 1959
CROOK, J. M. 'Sir Robert Smirke: a Pioneer of Concrete Construction', *Trans. Newcomen Soc.*, vol. xxxviii, 1965–66
DAVIS, A. C. *A Hundred Years of Portland Cement*, Concrete Publications, 1924
HALSTEAD, P. E. 'The early history of Portland cement', *Trans. Newcomen Soc.*, vol. xxxiv, 1961–62
SKEMPTON, A. W. 'Portland cements, 1843–87', *Trans. Newcomen Soc.*, vol. xxxv, 1962–63

SELECT BIBLIOGRAPHY

SPACKMAN, C. *Some Writers on Lime and Cement*, Helfer, 1929
THURSTON, A. P. 'Parker's Roman cement', *Trans. Newcomen Soc.*, vol. xix, 1939

Glass

BARKER, T. C. *Pilkington Brothers and the Glass Industry*, Allen & Unwin, 1960
CHADWICK, G. F. *The Work of Sir Joseph Paxton*, Architectural Press, 1961.
POWELL, H. J. *Glass Making in England*, Cambridge University Press, 1923

Iron and Steel

BANNISTER, T. 'The first iron-framed buildings', *Architectural Review*, April 1950
GLOAG, J. AND BRIDGWATER, D. *A History of Cast Iron in Architecture*, Allen & Unwin, 1948
JOHNSON, H. R. AND SKEMPTON, A. W. 'William Strutt's cotton mills, 1793–1813', *Trans. Newcomen Soc.*, vol. xxx, 1955–56
SKEMPTON, A. W. AND JOHNSON, H. R. 'The first iron frames', *Architectural Review*, March 1962
SUTHERLAND, R. J. M. 'The introduction of structural wrought iron', *Trans. Newcomen Soc.*, vol. xxxvi, 1963–64

Stone

ARKELL, W. J. *Oxford Stone*, Faber, 1947; or *The Geology of Oxford*, Oxford University Press, 1947
BENFIELD, E. *Purbeck Shop: A Stone Worker's Story of Stone*, Cambridge University Press, 1940
LEE, C. E. 'The Slate Industry and Transport in North-West Wales', *Trans. Newcomen Soc.*, vol. xxxiv, 1961–62
O'NEILL, H. *Stone for Building*, Heinemann, 1965
PURCELL, D. *Cambridge Stone*, Faber, 1967.
Report of the Committee on Quarries and Stone for the New Houses of Parliament, 1839
ROYAL INSTITUTE FOR BRITISH ARCHITECTS. *Sir Christopher Wren, A.D. 1632–1723*, 1923

SLEE, J. 'A disappearing craft: slate-making in the Cotswolds', *Country Life*, 6 November 1958

WATTS, A. M. 'The Portland Stone Quarries' *Proc. Dorset Archaeological and Natural History Society*, vol xii, 1891

WOOD, J. *Essay Towards a Description of Bath*, 1749

Wood

LATHAM, T. *Timber—its Development and Distribution*, Harrap, 1957

SJOSTROM, C. *Prefabrication in Timber*, English Joinery Manufacturers' Assoc., 1943

WOOD, A. D. AND LUNN, T. G. *Plywoods: their Development, Manufacture and Application*, Johnston, 1942

Index

Abbey Mills Pumping Station, 109
Aberdeenshire; granite quarries, 16–17
Aberthaw limestone, 47
Acts of Parliament, 3, 47, 94–5, 95–7
Adam brothers, 39, 44, 67, 70
Adams Patent stucco, 144
adhesives (for timber), 78–9
Aegis slates, 85
aggregates, 60
Aircraft industry; demand for plywood, 74
Albert Memorial, 16
Allen, Ralph, 21, 27, 106
Alton Towers: conservatories, 110
aluminium: as structural material, 81–4; early uses of, 81–2, 88; for components, 81–2, 88
apprenticeship, 11, 12–13
Arborite, 90
Arlesey early cement kiln, 51
asbestos, 84–5
asbestos-cement, 85–6, 88
Ashby-de-la-Zouch: brickworks, 29
Ashburnham, 107
ashlar, 26
Aspdin, Joseph, 48
asphalt, 86, 104
Associated Portland Cement Manufacturers' Association, 51
Athenaeum Club, 45
Atkinson's cement, 48
Avonmouth Docks, 25

Bacup: sandstone quarries, 20
Bailey, William, 32

Bakelite, 89
balloon frames: for timber housing, 73
Baltic pine, 75
Banqueting Hall, Whitehall, 106
barracks, 5, 8
Barry, Sir Charles, 67
baths, 41
Bath Stone, 20–3, 24, 106
Bath Stone Firms Limited, 22–3
Bauhaus, 68
Bedford Square, 44
Beer; stone quarries, 24
Bellhouse, E. T., 4
Bell Rock lighthouse, 17
Bery, Max, 56
Beverley, William, 49
bitumen, 86–7
Blue Pennant stone, 24
Bocking Mill, Essex, 80
Bodleian Library: use of aluminium, 82
Bothwell Park: stone quarries, 24
Bournville Garden City, 4, 105
Boots' factory, Nottingham, 68
Bowles, John, 62
Box: stone mines, 26
Brabazon Hangar, 83
Bradford, 110
Bramah, Joseph, 41
Brent, 108
Breslau; Centenary Hall, 56
bricks: kilns for, 31–3, 107–8; making of, 28–9, 31–6, 107–8; sizes of, 28, 29, 108; taxes on, 29–31; types of, 34, 35, 36, 108

115

INDEX

brickwork, examples of, 28, 107–8
Bridford: granite quarries, 15
bridges; timber, 74–5
Bridgwater; brick and tile making, 37
Brighton Pavilion, 41, 70
Bristol, 107
British Fibro-Cement, 85
British Plastics Federation, 88
British (Cast) Plate Glass Company, 63
British Precast Concrete Federation, 61
British Standard Code of Practice, 78
Broad-glass, 62
Bromley (Kent), 108
Broxbourne, 107
Brunel, Isambard Kingdom, 4–5, 74–5, 80
Brunel, Marc Isambard, 48
Buckingham Palace, 8–9
Builder, The, 17
builders; meeting customers' budgets, 1–2
building boards, 78, 79
building boom: in Victorian period, 2
building regulations, 94–7
building societies, 5–6
building workers; definition, 11–12
Bunning, James, 67
Burlington: slate quarries, 17
burnt ballast, 53
Burraton; dam, 15
Burton, Decimus, 45, 66, 109
Buxton, 108

Cambridge University Library: use of aluminium, 82
Campbell, Colin, 22
Carlton House Terrace, 44
Carlton Tower Hotel, 26
Carron Ironworks, 70
cast-iron: columns, 66, 69–70; components, 40, 70–1, 88, 109–10
Castle Drogo: granite mansion, 16
cellar lights, 68–9
cellular concrete, 57

cement: kilns for, 50–1; manufacture of, 49–50; types, 43–4, 47–52, 46–9, 101
Centenary Hall, Breslau, 56
Cézanne, Louis, 60
Chadwick, Sir Edwin, 3, 41
Châgres, 104
Chance, Henry, 62
Chance, Robert Lucas, 64–5
Chatham Dockyard: Boat Stores, 80
Chatsworth Conservatory, 64
Cheltenham Ladies College, 80
Cherbourg: harbour works, 49, 52
Chilmark, 106
Chilton Trinity: tilemaking, 37
Cité de Réfuge, Paris, 68
civic price: expressed in Victorian buildings, 2, 5
Civil engineering: need for hydraulic cement, 47
Civita Vecchia; pozzulana, 47
clay bricks and blocks, 59–60
clays (for brick-making), 31, 33
Clipsham, 23, 24, 106
Cluny: granite quarries, 17
Coade, George and Eleanor, 39
Coade Stone, 39–40, 107
Coal Exchange, 67
Cockerell, Sir Charles, 66
Cockermouth, Keswick and Penrith Railway, 16
Coggleshall Mill, 80
Coignet, François, 55
Collyweston: stone tiles, 19
Combe Down; quarries, 21
combination ranges, 70
commercial buildings; in Victorian period, 2
Compton Wynyates, 28
concrete: blocks, 58–9; development of, 51–3, 108–9; mixing and placing of, 55, 60; prestressed, 61; reinforced, 51, 53–7, 61; roofing tiles, 38; shuttering, 61; types of, 58, 60, 61; vibrators, 60
conservatories, 64–7

INDEX

construction workers; definition, 11–12; numbers of, 11–12
contracts, 8–9
Copenhagen railway station, 80
Cornwall Railway, 75
Cornwall: slate quarries, 17
Cornwood: railway viaduct, 15
corrugated iron, 67
Corsham, 106
craftsman, numbers of, 10–11, 12, 13
Craigleith: stone quarries, 25
Crompton, Thomas Russell, 51
Cronkbourne, 105
crown-glass, 62, 63
Crystal Palace, 65
Cubitt, William, 9
Cubitts (contractors), 9, 12
curtain-wall construction, 68, 109
cylinder glass, 62, 63–4

Daily Express building, 68
Dalton: sandstone quarries, 20
damp courses, 86
Dance, George, 52
Dartmoor granite, 14–15, 16, 106, 107
De Bijenkorf store, Rotterdam, 68
decay: in stone, 23; in timber, 80
Delabole: slate quarry, 17
de Morveau, Baron Louis Bernard Guyton, 48
Devonport Dockyard, 80
Dictionary of British Sculptors, 40
Dietsch kiln, 51
Dihl, Christopher, 44
Dischinger, Fritz, 61
Dorchester, 107
Doulting: quarries, 23
Doulton, Henry, 41
Doultons (of Lambeth), 39, 40–2
drains, 40–1
Drewsteignton: granite mansion, 16
Dudley: limekilns, 50; Museum, 50
Dunlop Cotton Mill, Castleton, 85

Early Victorian Architecture in Britain, 67

Eastwoods brickworks, 34
Edinburgh: stone quarries, 25
Eddystone lighthouse, 47
Edith Weston: stone quarries, 23
Ellesmere Canal, 48
Elslow: brickworks, 35
Empire Stadium, Wembley, 85
epoxide resins, 90
Eros statue, 81
Eyambo, King, 104

faience, 38
Fairbairn, Sir William, 53
Farquharson, Francis, 32
Festiniog: slate quarries, 17
fibreboard, 79
Fibreglass, 61, 91
Fibro tiles, 85
Fish Market (Charing Cross), 66
Fishponds, Bristol: stone, 24
FitzAlwyn's Assize (1189), 94
Fletton bricks, 33–4
Foggintor: granite quarry, 15
Forder brickworks, 34
Forest of Dean stone, 24–5
Formica, 90
Fox and Barrett floors, 53
Friends Provident offices, Bristol: use of aluminium, 81
framed buildings, 67–8
Freyssinet, Eugene, 56, 61

Gardner, George, 76
Gateshead: cement works, 49, 50
General Post Office, 52
Germany: cement production, 51
Gibbons, Grinling, 44
Giffnay, 106
Gilbert, Sir Alfred, 81
Gilfach slate quarry, 17
glass: bricks, 65, 69; cladding, 67–9; duty, 63–4; exports, 63; making of, 62; silk, 65; tax on, 63–5; toughened, 65, 69; types of, 62–3, 65–6, 68, 69; use with iron, 66–9
glazing techniques, 65, 67

Glencaise, 107
Gloucestershire stone, *see* Bath stone
Godwin, George, 52–3
government contracts, 8
granite: production of, 15–16; sources of, 14–17, 106–7; use of, 15–17
Grange, Alresford: conservatories, 66
Great Exhibition (1851), 3, 42, 65, 74
Great Fire (1666), 20, 94
Great Western Railway, 22
Greenwich Hospital, 22
gritstone, 20
Guinness, Robert, 40
gypsum plaster, 43

Hallidee Building, San Francisco, 68
Hamelin's Patent Cement, 44
Ham Hill: stone quarries, 23
Hammersmith Iron Works (Dublin), 66
Hampton Court Palace, 109
Hanover Square, 44
Harington, Sir John, 41
Hardwick Hall, 44
Harwich stones, 47–8
Haslingden: sandstone quarries, 106
Hatschek, Ludwig, 84–5
Hawksmoor and James, 22
Haytor: granite quarries, 15
Health of Towns and Populous Places, Report on (1847), 3
Hennebique, François, 56
Hitch, Caleb, 108
Hitchcock, Henry-Russell, 67
Hoffmann, Friedrich, 32
Hollow clay blocks, 59
Holt, Richard, 39
Horstead Mill, Norfolk, 80
house costs, 3, 5–7
household refuse: as material for concrete, 60
Housing Manual (1923), 11
housing standards, 3–5
Hurstmonceux, 28

hydraulic cement, 47
hydraulic lime, 46

industrial buildings, 2
Institute of British Architects, 9
Institution of Structural Engineers, 84
iron (for prefabricated buildings), 4–5, 104
ironmongery, builders', 75
Irving, William, 32
Isle of Wight: cement production, 48
Ivybridge: railway viaduct, 15

Jennings South Western Pottery, 42
jerry-building, 7–9
Johnson, I. C., 49
Jolliffe and Banks, 50
Jones, Inigo, 44

Keinton stone, 24
Kendal: lime kilns, 108
kerbs, 16, 17
Kemnay: granite quarries, 17
Kennet and Avon Canal, 22
Ketton: stone quarries, 23
Kew: Palm House, 66, 109
kiln-drying (of timber), 79–80
kilns: for brick-making, 31–3; for cement, 50–1
King's Cross Station, 6
Kodak factory, 69

Lake District: granite quarries, 16; slate quarries, 17
Lamberhurst: ironworks, 70
Lambot, Jean Louis, 54
laminated materials, 77–8, 90, 110
Lavenham: pargetting, 43
Layer Marney Towers, 28, 39
Laycock, William, 104
Le Corbusier, 68
Le Havre: Church of St Joseph, 57
Le Moulin Idéal, 56
Le Raincy: Church of Notre Dame, 57
Letchworth, 4
Liandet's stucco, 44

Lidlington brick works, 34
Lime Street Station, Liverpool, 67
lime, hydraulic, 46–7
lime-kilns, 50–1, 108–9
lime mortar, 46–7
limestone: production of, 23–4; sources of, 19–20, 106; uses of, 20, 23
Limmer rock-asphalt, 87
Lindisfarne: lime-kilns, 50
Lion Brewery symbol, 40, 107
Liscannor: sandstone quarries, 25
Little Castleton: stone quarries, 23
Liverpool Cotton Exchange, 71
loans, housing, 3
London Brick Company, 34
London Bridge, 15, 17
London Building Acts, 47, 95–7
London Potters' Association, 41
Lorraine: glass industry, 62
Lyme Regis: cement production, 48
Lynmouth: lime kilns, 108

Macclesfield: furniture store, 69
Maillart, Robert, 56
Marston Valley Brick Company, 34
Measham: brickworks, 108
measurement of work, 8, 9
Mechanick Exercises (1678), 45
Medina cement, 48
Medway: cement works, 49, 70
melamine formaldehyde, 90
Merrivale: granite quarries, 15, 16
Merstham: limeworks, 50; railway tunnel, 50
middle-class housing, 2, 5
millboard, 79
Millspaugh technique (asbestos cement), 33
millstone grit, 20, 25
Ministry of Reconstruction (1917), 4
Monier, Joseph, 54
Monks Park: stone mine, 26, 106
Montacute House, 107
Monymusk: granite quarries, 17
moorstone, 16
mortar, 46

Moxon, Joseph (quoted), 45–6
Mulgrave cement, 48
mushroom-slab construction, 56

nail and screw production, 73–4
Nash, John, 8–10, 44, 70
National History Museum, 39
Nature and Properties of Concrete, The, 52
Nelle factory, Rotterdam, 68
neoprene, 68
Nettlefold and Chamberlain, 74
Newcastle-upon-Tyne: glass industry, 62; reinforced concrete house, 54
New Lanark, 105
New Street Station, Birmingham, 67
Newgate Prison, 52
New York Building Code, 95
No-fines concrete, 57
Nonsuch Palace, 44
Nort: concrete mill building, 56
North Devon: lime-kilns, 50
Northfleet: cement works, 51
Nottingham: Boots' factory, 68
nylon, 90

Office of Works, 8
oil mastics, 44
Old Hardwick Hall, 44
oleaginous cements, 44
Orly airship hangars, 56–7

pantiles, 36
pargetting, 43
Paris Exhibition (1855), 54
Parker, James, 47
Parker's cement, 47–8
Parndon, 7
particle board, 78
Pasley, Sir Charles, 48
Patent Millboard Company, 79
pavement lights, 68–9
paving blocks, 16
Paxton, Sir Joseph, 64–5
payment systems in building industry, 8–9

INDEX

Peabody Trust, 3–4
Penitentiary (Millbank), 52
Perret, Auguste, 57
Perrot, Bernard, 63
Perspex, 89
Perstorp, 90
Peterhead: granite quarries, 17
Peter Jones Store, 68, 109
phenol formaldehyde, 90
phenolic resins, 79
phenolics, 90
Pilkington Bros, 63, 65–6, 109
Pioneer block-making machine, 59
Pitch Lake, Trinidad, 86
plaster of Paris, 43
plaster panels, 92–3
plasterboard, 91–3
plasterers' tools, 45–6
plastics: properties of, 89; reinforced, 91; types of, 89–91; uses of, 87–9
plate-glass, 62–3, 67–8
plywood, 76–7, 79
pollution of water supplies, 40
polystyrene, 90
polythene, 91
polyvinyl chlorides, 91
polyvinyl fluoride, 91
poor: housing for, 1, 3
population growth, 1, 3
Port Chester: reinforced concrete house, 54
Portland Place, 44
Port Sunlight, 4, 105
Portland cement, 48–9, 60
Portland stone, 20–2, 24, 25, 106, 107
pozzolanas, 46
prefabrication, 4–5, 26, 70–1, 82–4
Prince Consort, 40–1
Princetown: prison buildings, 15
Public Health Acts, 41, 97
Pulham, James, 107
Pulinge: brickworks, 34
pulpwood, 79

Queen's College, Cambridge, 26

Radcliffe Infirmary: use of aluminium, 83
Ragusa asphalt, 86
railways, iron, 70
railways: use of bricks, 30; use of timber bridges, 74–5
rainwater goods, 88
Randall and Saunders, 22
Ransome, Frederick, 51, 56
Ravenhead glassworks, 63
Rawtenstall: sandstone quarries, 20
reconstituted stone, 26
Report on Building Stones for the New House of Commons, 23
Report on the Structural Use of Aluminium Alloys in Buildings, 84
Redland (Flettons) Limited, 34
Reed, Ezekiel, 73
Regent's Park Terrace, 10, 44
reinforced concrete, *see under* concrete, reinforced
Reinforced Concrete Centenary (Paris 1948), 54
resorcinal formaldehyde resins, 79
Revel: early plywood manufacture, 76
Rhineland: glass industry, 62
Rhiwback slate quarry, 18
Ripley, Thomas, 39
Ritz Hotel, 97, 109
rock-asphalt, 86–7
Rolt, L. T. C., 74–5
Roman cement, 46–8
rooflights, 69
roofs, large-span, 56
rotary kiln, 51
Royal Botanical Society conservatory, 66
Royal Commission on the Housing of Working Classes, 3
Royal Cornwall Institution, 75
Royal Exchange, 67
Royal Mail Steam Packet Co., 104
Rubber and Plastics Research Association, 88
Rubislaw: granite quarries, 17
Rutland: stone quarrying, 23

St Paul's Cathedral, 70
St George's Hall, Newport, 20
St Martin-in-the-Fields, 70
St Osyth's Priory, 28
St Ouen: concrete factory, 56
Sackett, Augustus, 91
Saclay: Atomic Energy Research Centre, 57
Sandringham: concrete tennis court, 55
San Gioacchino, Rome: aluminium roofing, 81
sandstone: production of, 25; sources of, 19–20, 25; uses of, 20, 25
sanitary pipeware and pottery, 40–2
sawmills, 75–6
Scheveningen: houses of no-fines concrete, 58
School of Military Engineering, Chatham, 48
Scotland: granite quarries, 16–17; slate quarries, 17
Scott, Sir Giles Gilbert, 81
screw-making, 73–4
septaria, 47
sett-making, 16
sewers, 40
Shaftesbury, Lord, 3
Shamrock stone, 25
Shand, Morton, 66
Shap: granite quarries, 16, 107
Sheppey stones, 47–8
Shopping arcades, 66
shuttering, 61
sink, kitchen, 41–2
slate: production of, 17–18; sources of, 17; tiles, 18–19, 38
slums, 3, 6
Smeaton, John, 46, 49
Smirke, Sir Robert, 52
Society of Arts, 75
Somerset Trading Company, 37
South Devon: lime-kilns, 50
South Owram: stone quarry, 25
Southwark Bridge, 25
staircases, cast-iron, 70
Stanley Mill, 110

Stansfield, James, 75–6
Staple Tor: granite quarries, 16
steam engines: for builders' plant, 6
steel, 67, 95
Stewart, Sir Hailey, 34
Stewart, Sir P. Malcolm, 34
Stewartby, 34–5, 108
stock-bricks, 36
Stokes, Frederick, 51
stone, building, 14, 25–7 *see also under specific types*
stone industry, growth of, 20
Stonesfield: stone tiles, 19
stone tiles, 19, 38
stoneware, 40–2
Structural Use of Aluminium in Building, Report on, 84
stucco, 10, 44
Sutherland, D. M., 79
Syon House, 39, 66, 109
Swadlincote, 108
Swanscombe: cement works, 49
Swell Tor: granite quarries, 15
Swindon: housing, 5–6, 105–6; railway works, 80
Syon House: conservatories, 66

Tamar: lime-kilns, 50
tarras mortar, 46–7
Tavarnasa Bridge, 56
tea-chests, 77
technical colleges, 12–13
Telford, Thomas, 48
Temple Meads station, 80
tenders, 7
tenements, 3–4
terracotta, 38–9
textile mills, 70
Tietz store, Berlin, 67–8
Thaxted: pargetting, 43
thiokol, 68
Thirlmere waterworks, 16
tiles: manufacture of, 30, 36–7, 104; taxes on, 29–30; types of, 36, 38; uses of, 29, 37–8
timber: adhesives for, 78–9; decay in, 80; for bridges, 73–4;

sawmills, 75–6; seasoning of, 79; types of, 76–8; uses of, 72–3, 77–8, 80, 110; veneers, 76
timber house types, 73
Tinworth, George, 39
Todmorden: mill, 69–70
Toulon: harbour, 52
trade unions, 12–13
transit concrete mixers, 60
Troy Court, London, 68
Trafford tiles, 85
training courses, 12–13
Turner, Richard, 66–7, 109
Turner Brothers, 85

United Services Club, 44
urea formaldehyde: glues, 78–9; mouldings, 96

Val de Travers asphalt, 87
Veneers, 76
Victoria, Queen, 41
Victorian building boom, 2–4

Wales: slate quarries, 17–18
Walker, Mr, of Poplar, 104
Walker Art Gallery, 20
Waltham Abbey, 28
Wapping-Rotherhithe tunnel, 48
Ward, William E., 54
Ware, 108
Warerite, 90
Wark, David, 44
water closets, 41
water pipes, 40
Waterloo Bridge, 52

Wayss: concrete structure by, 56
weatherboard cladding, 80
Welbeck: Riding School, 66
Welwyn Garden City, 4
Wembley: Empire Pool, 109
Western Beacon: granite quarries, 15
West-India Docks, 17
Westmorland: slate quarries, 17–18
Weymouth Bay: cement production, 48
What is to become of Crystal Palace?, 65
Whitbread's Brewery, 110
Whitby cement, 48
Widnes: manufacture of asbestos cement, 85
Whiteley's store, 69
Wilkes, Sir Joseph, 29, 108
Wilkes' Gobs (bricks), 29, 108
Wilkinson, W. B., 54–5
window-frames, iron, 70
window-tax, 64
Wood, Eric S., 50
working-class housing, 1–3, 5, 7
workmanship standards, 7–10, 23
Wren, Sir Christopher, 44
wrought iron, 53, 69–70
Wyatt, Job and William, 73

Yeo: granite working, 16
York Minster, 39
Yorkshire cement, 48
York stone, 25

Zurich: Maillart warehouse, 56